Crying Without Tears

CINDY SPRAY

For permission requests and ordering information, email the publisher at:
info@twopennypublishing.com

ISBN: 978-1-950995-24-0
eBook also available

FIRST EDITION

For more information about the author or to book an event appearance or media interview, please contact the author representative at:
info@twopennypublishing.com or visit cryingwithouttears.com

DISCLAIMER: Although this publication is designed to provide accurate information in regard to the subject matter covered, the publisher and the author assume no responsibility for errors, inaccuracies, omissions, or any other inconsistencies herein. This publication is meant as a source of valuable information for the reader, however it is not meant as a replacement for direct expert assistance. If such level of assistance is required, the services of a competent professional should be sought.

Contents

Dedication

The decision to whom I would dedicate this book was made well before it was written. I dedicate it to my sister, Donna Jean. During her short years on this earth, she suffered from so many forms of child abuse, depression, and issues from adult relationships that she could not overcome.

Suicide is hard on those who are left behind and the survivors who ask themselves what they could have done differently. It never goes away. She visits and talks to me occasionally, in my dreams.

God forgave you Donna for taking your own life. He welcomed you into his kingdom so you could have the peace you truly deserved. You found it in heaven! I love you, Donna.

National Suicide Prevention Lifeline
Hours: Available 24 hours
800-273-8255

5

Acknowledgments

All of those who have touched me throughout my life, I carry a piece of you with me, always. People who gave me the courage to share my story to have an impact on others gave me the passion for writing this book.

To my husband, Dave, my daughter Renee Crowder, my sons Anthony and Jason Crowder. They have respected me and genuinely accepted me for who I am. The love and gratitude I have for my family runs deep in my soul and they support me in all I do.

I want to thank my younger sister Cathy Elaine. She and I have had many conversations where we share our youth sibling memories of the few years we grew up together. Her words resonate with me in ways that only she and I can understand. I love you, sissy!

To Betty Spelman, a mentor who took me under her wings to teach me about the bookkeeping field. She is a person whom I admire greatly who helped alter the course of my adult life.

It is my honor to recognize Vanessa Adkins. Your one act of kindness as my classmate has led to a lifetime of friendship, sharing memories and I thank you for being there for me.

I must thank my dearest friend Charlotte Madar for her tireless, never-ending commitment to this endeavor. Her humor and multitude of facial expressions during the countless hours we spent together is what kept me motivated to write. I cannot thank her enough, and I will always cherish our friendship.

Eternally Grateful,
Cindy Spray

Introduction

As a child, I had no choices in my future. Yet, GOD chose me to be the protector of my brothers and sisters. I had to make critical decisions that affected my entire family. I decided to protect my youngest family members from a life I was already living.

I went from being the most hated member of the family to the most respected. Through it all, God held my hand and my heart. He led my life. Through God, I found healing, hope, joy, and strength.

I didn't write this story. I lived it! More importantly, I survived it because...

"God had a path for me long before I ever knew it."

As you travel through this journey, you will discover that even cases of common disease and illnesses were huge battles I had to overcome. But, even that would be just a sampling of the pain and suffering I was going to have to rise above. Strength was not something I was taught. I had to learn how to become healthy and find my own strength among the madness. I learned how to navigate through difficult situations as I protected the most vulnerable within my own family.

I was forced to live a life of *Crying Without Tears*. Now, my path is to share my story and be the voice for those who struggle through their adult life after child abuse. You are not alone, and I will be your voice and the voice for children. We need to bring awareness to this continual cycle. Recognize the signs that abused children are giving—I showed many signs over the years that went unnoticed. Listen to what their eyes are saying.

chapter one

Family Matters

My grandmother was the rock of my mom's family. She often bragged about the large number of grandchildren she had; she was a proud grandma and a stern matriarch. She had worked as a nanny for one of our local physicians, and on occasion, she would take me along. The physician had two girls close to my age, and the three of us became friends. Gram would do the laundry and iron the pillowcases as they came out of the clothes dryer while the girls and I played.

Sewing was one of her specialties. She had a sewing machine set up in her house all of the time. It was worn from constant use. I would watch her sew, cook, and I would listen to her recite the names of her many cactus plants as we walked through the different rooms of her house to water them. She always told us kids, not to touch them. Naturally, I was as tempted as any kid would be and stuck my finger out too far. Sure enough, I got stuck by the thorns. Gram had to get her tweezers and pull the nasty little prickles out of my finger, all while scolding me, "I told you so." From then on, my curiosity in cacti was satisfied and I kept my distance from them.

We never knew our grandparents on my dad's side of the family. His mother died while giving birth to him, leaving his father (my grandpa) widowed. Dad's siblings were older and took care of themselves, while distant relatives were raising dad. We had a minimal relationship with dad's side of the family. Anytime we would collectively visit their homes, the kids would have to stay out in the yard or inside the car. Mom later told me it was because they thought they were better than us and did not want any of her kids to break the finer things they kept in their home. The exception was the uncle who bounced from house to house, never owning more than what was in the front seat of his pickup truck.

To paint a picture of my mom and dad is difficult. In my case, it was their role of being the adults in the house. For me, there is a monumental difference between being a parent or simply being called a mother or father. It was just mom and dad, and I became the protector–a guardian–if you will, of my younger siblings. I had to adapt to the life I was given, discover, and create different ways to protect my siblings from the violence in our home. In reality, at an early age, a tremendous amount of responsibility landed on my shoulders.

Mom and dad never spent any quality time with any of us. They just kept producing kids that they could not afford to raise financially or morally. Mom was a petite woman who looked like she had a basketball under her clothing all the time, walking around with 'one on the way,' as they say. I thought she was pretty, and when I asked her why she wore her long black hair up in a ponytail or a bun, she told me, "it's to keep it out of my face and to prevent the kids from pulling it." Looking back at it all, I would say she wore it up so my dad could not grab onto it in the heat of the arguments they had.

She was completely addicted to unfiltered cigarettes, coffee, and soap operas. Oh, the drama of the soap operas! As though she needed to watch them—our family had a real-life drama that she chose to ignore. She would have me light her cigarettes on the burner of the gas stove. Obviously, as a little girl, I didn't know how to light a cigarette, so I would hold it to a flame to light it. I would run it back to her, and she would yell at me in disgust if it would go out.

Then she would make me do it again, telling me, "Puff on it to make it light!" So, I slightly puffed on it until the end of it would glow bright enough to stay lit. I can remember the paper sticking to my lips as I pulled it out of my mouth to hand it to her. The taste of the tobacco in my mouth was impossible to forget. The effects of the nicotine would linger in my body.

Another chore of mine was to make her countless cups of instant coffee as she sat in front of the TV all day watching her favorite soap operas. She didn't want to miss a moment of the breathtaking drama about to unfold in a thrilling new episode that she was watching. During the commercials, she would rush to the outhouse to do her business then rushed back inside, fearful of missing one moment of the suspense. Those trips to the outhouse were the fastest I ever saw her move. Looking back, I can only shake my head, thinking that this was her perception of a normal life.

Mom began physically abusing her children. Two of my brothers and one of my sisters were her main targets. She would get very violent with them, punching them with her fist clenched so tightly that her knuckles were white. She would hit them so hard that she hurt herself. Then, she would shake out her fist and punch them again. She became so mad while hitting them and would blame them for 'hurting her.' She would kick and repeatedly beat them for the smallest of reasons; perhaps sometimes, she didn't even have a valid reason.

Countless times she called them names and yelled at them, saying, "I hate your damn guts." If really mad—which was often— she would add, "I wish you were never born." To a child, nothing could be worse than a mom telling her kids that she hated them. Worse yet, that she wished she had never had them at all.

My sister Donna Jean was a tomboy. She was the kind of girl who did not back down from anything or anybody, including our mom. She would get herself into so much trouble for talking back whenever she was told to do something, and then proceed to tell Mom, "No, make Cindy do it." Our 'mom' was the kind of person who expected her kids to do what they were told; otherwise, she would take quick action that was most often physical. It was her way of retaliation I believe. She often said to us, "if you don't listen to me, you'll be sorry."

Mom's typical response to one of us 'talking back' was simple and swift.

She would furiously rise from her chair, charge toward us, and display such hate and anger. Whichever kid was defying her, she would knock them to the floor. It was easier for me to do what I was told.

In one of these incidents, I remember Mom stomping on Donna's face and body as she rolled across the floor to try to dodge mom's feet. Mom was alternating from one foot to the other, trying to get better aim and to keep her balance as she stomped to do more harm. I would yell at Donna in an attempt to get mom to settle down. "Donna, be quiet! Shut up so she will stop beating you," I would say, as I tried to get her away from our mom's range and field of vision. In our house, 'out of sight and out of mind' was a wonderful thing. Sometimes it worked, but many times not. I could feel the pain that Donna was suffering. The possibility of broken ribs during one of these violent outbursts was never out of the question.

Heartbreakingly, even my two younger brothers were the object of Mom's rage. Sadly, but fortunately, they were small enough for me to pick them up and get them out of her way. I taught them to behave, so they would not draw attention to themselves when she became enraged, ill-willed, and violent. It didn't take long for the little ones to recognize the signs of anger.

We all took her verbal abuse, but the little ones counted on me to get them out of mom's way as fast as possible. I don't know if anyone can imagine being treated like that, but I felt it, heard it, and witnessed it many times. In all, I lived it. I always did my best to step in and redirect her anger towards me and separate them from her. I can't imagine what went on during school days with the babies and the younger kids that were left in her care. I'm sure that when they interfered with her daily TV activities, they paid for it. I would often see a new bruise where one didn't exist the day before.

Dad had a violent temper that was usually directed at our mom. I wondered if he was angry with her because she wouldn't take responsibility for the basic needs of her kids. His rage often led him to physically abuse her. I never understood why she treated us poorly and took no real interest in any of us. She continued to neglect and abuse us, and our dad was certainly no better than her.

There were times when I saw my dad hit my younger brother with whatever might be in arm's reach. A broom handle was a common weapon for my dad to grab. He would chase my brother out the door, hitting him in the back and on his arms, and even on the back of his head. I still don't know why my dad targeted my younger brother. He might have seen his own traits in my brother.

Some parents unwittingly favor one child over another, treating them a bit better than the rest. My family was no different in having a favorite. But, mom and dad also had their favorites to beat on and abuse. Years later, I reflect on many of the episodes that unfolded.

"I remember the house, the broom, the bruises, every little detail."

There were so many things wrong and evil about this man— my 'dad'—that I cannot write about all of it. My aunts and uncles often talked about how out of control he would act for no reason at all, sometimes at the drop of a hat. It did not take much to set him off, and as kids, we feared him. Early on, I feared him far more than the others. I saw him differently. Some loved him, some did not, but then again, what is real affection? We did not know.

Mom and dad often got in terrible screaming fights. Mom would cry and try to protect herself from being hit. My brother would scream at my dad, "Stop! Leave her alone," as my mom used her hands to cover and protect her face. The fights were common and were always chaotic.

The younger kids were always scared, crying, and running all over the place to get away from the horror. I would gather them up and take them into a separate room so that they wouldn't see the violence and total mayhem, but they could still hear it. I would start singing to them, "Twinkle, twinkle, little star, do you know how sweet you are." That's what I had to do in order to calm them down and try to distract them from the madness that was always around us. The louder our mom and dad yelled and screamed at each other, the louder I would sing. They still cried in fear, and many times I would lie on the floor with them until they would fall asleep.

I did not know it as I lived it, but God was preparing me to become a stronger person, to deal with some difficult trials that were about to come into my life. As if I didn't already have enough to challenge me. Early on, there was a path that I did not see. It would become a path of living hell—a place where strength became the very essence of my life. When we are given a path, we must trust in God and listen to those little whispers in our hearts to know which direction to go.

"Because God had a path for me, long before I ever knew it!"

chapter two

The Scars Left Behind

Who knew that I would be the one who would change the makeup of our entire family. I would discover new directions, and find real love, respect, and hope in others. I wanted to have a positive impact on others and make a difference as I went through life. I wanted to have self-worth and feel like I had value. It was something we did not have in my family. I didn't know if it even existed.

I could not rely on my family who did not offer anything but despair and sadness. I often looked around and saw what I would become if I followed in their footsteps. I did not want their lifestyle to become my future. I had different dreams! What would it take to break the pattern of years of never-ending cycles of the same behaviors within my family? The alcoholic uncle, members who were mentally challenged, and those who committed sexual abuse. So many unanswered questions.

I wondered what started this kind of cycle in my family. I couldn't figure it out because I had not seen this behavior in my grandmother's life or in her household. The woman who raised my mom, three other girls, and a son, all of who became terrible parents in one form or another. The despicable parenting methods, the beating of their kids, sending them to bed at 5 o'clock because they didn't want to look at their faces for the rest of the night. The multiple puncture wounds from a spanking with a wired hairbrush on a cousin's bottom during potty training.

For me, I took notice when I was old enough and saw that some of the kids who came on the first day of the new school year were holding their bags of new school supplies. My family had to use the broken crayons left behind from the students who moved onto the next grade level. At times, we were given donated supplies that had been collected throughout the community. Often, they included a little box of only eight crayons. But, I wanted to be like the kids with a big set of 64 crayons with a sharpener on the box! But, well before crayons became a goal for me, I would have other battles to fight. So, let the battles begin!

The earliest age I can remember vividly is four because so many illnesses had already started and seemed to be never-ending as I grew older. I was one of the frailest of the children who always seemed to be sick with something. One of the worst instances of being sick was having to be hospitalized with scarlet fever. Although I was too young to understand the medical terminology, I somehow understood the severity of this illness.

The staff questioned my mom about the history of her family's health. We already knew that her twin brother had died from this disease. It was a common outcome with this illness. My mom and her twin brother were six years old at the time of his death, so there was a great deal of concern that I might not survive it.

A few days later, the staff had requested the hospital Chaplain to come to my room and pray over me, a practice they had in place when patients were severely ill. I was in a stainless-steel crib with an ankle tied to one of the rods. It was what was done in effort to keep toddlers from getting out. I did not have the strength to climb out, but it was routine. The fever was so high that I can remember how dry my mouth was, how hard it was for me to swallow, and to open my eyes to see anyone who entered the room.

One afternoon, I felt as if every ounce of life was leaving my little body. I may have been taking the last few fighting breaths I had left. I don't know if that was the case, but I remember the weakness so well. It was as if I was allowing myself to die that day. Until, a very regal man came into my room wearing a dark suit. He had a Bible in one hand, and he was carrying a white teddy bear in the other! The size of teddy bears you win at a fair, or at least it seemed that big to me. Some of the staff, some family members, including my mom, followed behind him as he entered the room. Still, it was the Chaplain and teddy bear that caught my attention—a welcomed sight for a child who was so ill.

When he put the teddy bear into my crib, I began to snuggle and caress the softness of it as he opened the Bible to a page bookmarked with a satin ribbon that tailed out at the bottom edge of his Bible. He began reading words, then placed his hand on my forehead and said words like "Dear God in heaven, as I stand here and pray." I did not know what he was doing or what prayer was. My attention was focused on the teddy bear because it was providing me with real comfort when I needed it most.

The voices began to fade as I drifted off to sleep with my arms around the teddy bear. I will never forget that moment because it was my first encounter with faith. Even though I didn't understand it, I somehow felt it.

"I remember the room, the teddy bear, the Chaplain, every little detail!"

Days later, I began to regain my strength, stand up in the crib, talk, and play with the bear. I was sent home a few days later with the bear and a few other gifts the nurses had given me. A short-lived recovery as I soon faced another illness that was circulating among my family. The German Measles!

We were living in a small house on Dodge Street when I had

scarlet fever. While my body began to recover, my grandmother kept me at her home to protect me from the disease. No one in the entire family was allowed to come and visit, but I still became severely infected with it anyway and was taken home to my mom, only to discover how cruel she could be.

The rash and fever that came with the measles were terrible. I would violently throw up. Mom, being the kind of person she was, forced me to clean up my vomit with newspapers as I continued to throw up. I tried doing what she said, even in the sickly state I was in, with the rash covering my entire body. She continued to yell at me as I tried to circle the newspapers in a way that would soak up the mess. I had to carry the dripping newspapers to a trash bin several times, and use a dry mop to clean what was left behind.

I remember my mom and aunt having conversations about why the disease seemed to be more severe with me than the rest of the kids. But I was no ordinary kid, and was becoming stronger and stronger the older I became. I would have to learn how to stand on my own two feet time and time again.

One spring we had gone to a cabin along the riverside where an uncle was staying. It was a beautiful quiet setting in a wooded area. Our uncle had a small campfire where the adults stood around and talked as I poked the fire with some of the smaller sticks and threw in some dried leaves to watch it smoke. My uncle had fishing line and hooks and told us to find a stick to fish with. So, I wandered off to find a branch to use as a fishing pole while the smaller kids began to dig in the dirt using spoons to find worms for bait.

A day or so later, a different kind of rash appeared on my thigh. It was more blistering than ordinary poison ivy. As a child who seemed to get minor rashes all the time, I knew this was not the typical type of rash. As the days went by, the blisters became bigger and had spread to another spot on the opposite thigh. They were getting huge and started popping up in various areas on my legs. The swelling increased the size of my thighs so much it became extremely difficult to walk. The rash was going deeper into the layers of my skin and down into the muscles! It soon caused me to limp, step by step, until I could not walk at all. I had to be carried to the outhouse during the day and was given a cup to pee in at night.

This rash was progressing rapidly and was getting so bad my legs became useless. My grandmother demanded that my mom and dad take me to the doctor. At this point, they had no choice.

Dr. McClure was his name. Why I can remember that I don't know, but I do. Upon examination, he found that the rash had gotten into the third level of muscle tissue on my thighs. He gave us a sample of a product in a box that looked like scotch tape. The directions were to put a piece of tape over the infected areas. The tape had a deep penetrating medication on it that would turn white as the medicine worked into the deeper layers of my legs.

It was the weirdest thing I ever witnessed, but it worked. To get the full effect of the treatment, the bandage had to be changed when it began to fall off. Once the sample box of tape had started to run out, my grandmother gave my mom and dad money to buy more of the prescription to keep the treatment going. Soon, the blisters began to dry up. My thighs had become as big as an adult's thigh from the swelling and redness.

Today when I look at the now diminished scars on my legs, it reminds me of the pain I went through with poison oak. But visible scars were constantly being replaced with those that could not be seen. Deep scars that we as individuals allow to haunt us, or we find the strength we need to overcome them, which I did time and time again. The kids depended on me. I did what I could to help them, not just because I was told to. I helped them because I truly loved them.

chapter three

Cheaper by the Dozen

Ultimately, our mom gave birth to a dozen kids! Can you imagine being pregnant that many times? Pamela Sue, one of the 12 she delivered, died during childbirth. I remember mom going to the hospital and later coming home without a baby. I was young, and I don't remember a grieving period at all—no tears or emotional distress from mom or dad. I know there had been a burial because we went to her gravesite once. I remember looking at the headstone. It didn't occur to me at the time that her dates of birth and death were the same day. When my oldest sister and I went back as adults, we finally made the connection.

The span between kids is so close that my brother and I are the same age for 15 days every year!! He used to boldly claim he was the oldest when we were younger, but now, I brag about being younger by 350 days! With all those brothers and sisters, I ultimately became known as the RUNT. Out of 11 kids in my family, a multitude of cousins, and my children, I am still the RUNT. Let me say that there are a lot of disadvantages to being short, but it also has advantages. For example, I can look eye to eye with most people when they are sitting down and, in group pictures, I'm placed in the front so I can be seen.

Being third in the "upper tier" of kids, as we called it, I was the one who always did what was asked of me. I never wanted to get into trouble or get a whipping, unlike my younger sister Donna often did. However, I did get into trouble here and there. On one specific occasion, some of my cousins and I were caught jumping on my mom and dad's bed. My dad yanked off his leather belt, doubled it over, and began whipping all of us. Somehow the buckled end of the belt slipped out of his hand, hitting me several times. It caused me to bleed and bruised my body in several areas. I was kept inside the house for many days and not allowed to go outside to play because the neighbors might see the huge belt marks that couldn't be hidden by clothing!

As soon as I was old enough to lift a baby, it became a big responsibility to help with the kids, especially the crawling babies and toddlers. I had to make bottles and change the nasty diapers my mom didn't want to change. We used the big diaper pins with the yellow ducks and pink chicks on them. Sometimes, the diapers would fall off the toddlers when they walked, so I would have to chase them and fix their diapers. I have many fond memories of them laughing and giggling at me as I chased them through the house. Yes, there was the occasional pin stick, and they would cry. But I was just a kid, and I felt terrible about it. Even more so if I made them bleed.

In a poor family the more kids you had, the more benefits you would get. With that many people in our family, we were given a huge stack of food stamps the first of the month. Mom and dad would buy stuff by the dozen. Dozens of loaves of bread, a few dozen pot pies, several dozen bags of dried beans, a dozen sacks of cornmeal, and a few 5-pound bags of basic flour. The self-rising variety was more expensive!

By the end of the month, when almost all the food had been eaten, we wouldn't have a lot of food left, but we would often have flour. We created a meal that became known to us as "HOBO BREAD." What the heck is "HOBO BREAD?" you might ask. It's quite simple. It's just a mixture of flour and water made into a dough. We would mash it out flat on the flour-covered table, then fry it in an iron skillet, browning it lightly with white commodity lard. It was a special treat if there was butter to put on top, but most of the time, we ate it plain.

During the holiday season, we would wait patiently for the "Good Fellows," a local charity organization that would bring us food, fruits, and toys at Christmas. While growing up, we didn't go visit a Santa Claus or make a list to mail. To us, the "Good Fellows" was our Santa and what we would get from them is what gave us our Christmas joy.

Even today, the smell of freshly peeled oranges and the taste of sliced fresh apples reminds me of Christmas and the "Good Fellows." They were kind volunteers who made Christmas brighter for the poorest of families.

They gave us these huge bags of walnuts, and I would watch our mom use a nutcracker to open them. It was my job to use a metal pick to pull out the nuts and fill a bowl. My aunts would come over with their bags of goodies and made it a family event picking out the nuts, peeling apples, and potatoes in preparation for a holiday feast. They would use the apples, walnuts, and marshmallows to make "apple salad" for our huge family Christmas dinner. Even though I went through some of the most difficult times, I do have a few good memories.

I dearly loved my grandmother. One of her trademarks was her ability to have a cigarette gripped tightly between her teeth while maintaining the entire length of ashes of the cigarette intact all the way to the butt. She always had a chain of safety pins on her blouse or on the dress that she would wear. Throughout the day, she would add to it, collecting them from different spots in the house. By evening, the strand would be down to her waistline.

She had so many talents she shared with the family, but to me, her sewing was special. My fondest memories of her were the clothes she made for me. She would reuse fabric from old bedsheets and old dresses that were stained while cooking or torn on the nail where the fly swatter hung near the sink.

During first grade, my family lived close to her and I attended school just blocks from her house. I would go to Grams house for lunch, and she would have a sandwich made and an Oreo cookie just off to the side of the plate. She asked me to take off my school dress so I wouldn't get it dirty while I ate.

While eating my lunch and dangling my feet under the seat of the chair, I listened to the sounds of her sewing machine stop and start, and the snips of the scissors here and there. She seemed to always have some type of sewing project.

Once, while I was sitting at the table in my undershirt and underwear, she made me a simple sleeveless blue dress with loops of satin ribbon sewn along the hemline. After grandma washed off my face, she slipped the dress over my head as I guided my hands through the armholes. She said I had to get back to school before the bell rang. I ran back across the schoolyard proud as a peacock in my brand-new, handmade dress my grandmother had just finished making moments ago.

The teacher noticed I was wearing something different than when I had left. She began complimenting me on how cute it was. I smiled with great pride, explaining that my grandma had just made it for me while holding out the hemline to show her the ribbon trim, which looked like an "L's" to me. Were there a dozen little "L's" on it? Who knows, but grandma bought stuff by the dozen too.

I wore that blue dress all the time because it was something special my grandmother had done for me, and no one else in school had a dress like it. However, that memory would be crushed forever in just a few short months.

chapter four

Nasty Nesting

We lived in some of the smallest, nastiest houses most families would not live in. It was necessary to take whatever we could afford. This meant the cheap rent places on dirt roads with only a bedroom or two, and in some cases not even a real heating system. A fan in a window to cool the house during the hot and humid summer days and nights was the only way of cooling the house. The one and only fan we had usually ended up in the same room our mom and dad slept in. Furnishings consisted of a full-size bed which would be set up in the living room of most of the houses we lived in, along with the black and white TV, a small couch, and an end table with an overflowing ashtray full of cigarette butts. A baby bed would be pushed into the corner for easy access in the middle of the night for my mom. A lot of activities took place in that room. It was a baby-making room, a nursery, and a TV room for the kids in between.

The cooking stove had splatters of food all over it, including some that had boiled over into the catch pans, which had blackened beneath the flames of the burners. I never knew they were supposed to be shiny. I didn't know that they could be removed, so when I cleaned the stove, I didn't even try to clean them. It was so bad that at times the catch pans would catch on fire while cooking. We turned off the gas burner, moved the pot over to blow out the flame and continue to cook on a lower setting. The amount of burnt food that was on the bottom of the oven and the grated shelves was equally as bad.

Our refrigerator in the corner of the kitchen had a stack of assorted bowls and loaves of sliced bread on top. We kept the loaves of bread on top of the refrigerator to keep the cockroaches from getting to them. Many times, even though the bugs would be scattered inside the bag, it was fed to us anyway. After all, what harm could a bug do to a piece of bread? The fridge was typically empty by the end of the month, along with the freezer section, which was used to store ten-cent pot pies bought with our allotted food stamps. The ice inside the freezer would get so thick, the metal ice cube trays would disappear in the snow like frost. When the food was gone, we would defrost and clean it out for the arrival of goods with the next massive food stamp buy. I would wipe out the refrigerator sections here and there, but broken eggs with yellow yokes and shells that had dried up along with other crusty foods required much more effort, which I never wanted to do. But, my mom would force me to do it a few days before the big shopping spree came.

Our floors would get so much dirt and mud on them that we had to use pancake turners to scrape it off. Guess who did that job? Me the RUNT, of course! We all had to chip in and do a lot of the many tasks it took to keep a path cleared out, which was a narrow walkway from the front door to the kitchen, up the stairs, to the back door, and the porch.

Our furniture was typically stained with food, baby pee, and so much dirt that the floral patterns were barely noticeable. We shared our space and furniture with cockroaches, mice, and insects that would often bite us, leaving marks on our bodies while we slept. Rats were common inside and outside of the houses in which we lived.

At night, kids would pile up on two or three beds, most often set up in the same room to share— if we had them at all. If I slept on a bed, I would be forced to sleep in the middle between two of my sisters, and I hated feeling closed in but didn't have to fight for the covers nor did I control them. Blankets were rare in our household and were something you claimed as yours when they were given to you.

Most of the time, we would just find a spot on the floor, use a pile of clothing as a pad to sleep on and towels or whatever we could find to cover up with. Sleeping near the potbelly stove in the winter was always a premium spot! The thin "covers" we did have offered little protection from the winter winds that created snowdrifts inside the cracks of the outer walls and around the doors that we had to slam shut to try to protect us from the cold.

At one house we lived in, there were two bedrooms upstairs. One of the A-frame rooms was unfinished with planked wooden flooring, a roof with similar planking across the truss boards, and walls with exposed wall studs and no insulation. It was one of the coldest areas in the house, but it was a place to hide among the mounds of clothes, a lot of junk, and a bare wired bed spring that laid in the middle of the floor. A pile of clothes on something besides the hard floor offered a bit of softness and comfort, if I piled it thick enough to cover the wire coils. That bed spring gave me a place to sleep even in the coldest of months when others were by the wood-burning stove. I hated that room because it felt so spooky, but it offered solitude when I needed it.

What I can only describe as a small couch or oversized chair was a great resting spot, and the place to watch television without having to sit on the floor with your legs crossed. It was a favorite spot that all of us kids wanted to park in. However, when an adult came into the room, we would be quickly shoved out of the way to allow them to occupy the seat.

One evening I was determined to claim that special chair

before anyone else did, so I held one of the babies in my arms to get them to fall asleep. Once asleep, I laid the baby behind my legs on the opposite side so they would not fall off in the middle of the night. I balled up a shirt that was lying on the floor to prop up my head and used the baby's blankets to cover us both.

I began to doze off to sleep, listening to whatever was being telecast on TV. In the middle of the night, I suddenly felt a tremendous pain deep inside my ear. I jumped up and yelled, "It hurts, it hurts, something is in my ear." I screamed out, trying to wake my mom, who was sleeping on the bed that was set up in the living room and was right next to me. I kept on saying it to try to get the attention of my mom or dad to help me. Mom finally raised her head from the pillow, and told me to be quiet and go back to sleep saying she would look at it in the morning.

I thought it might have been a cockroach that crawled into my ear as I slept. I didn't know what I could do to help myself, and my mom wasn't at all interested in looking at it until morning. I heard this thing shuffling inside my ear as it moved around the rest of the night. The sounds and the pain kept me up as I bounced my head on the arm of the chair, trying to get it to come out with no success. I waited and waited for daylight to come so she could look at it and try to do something.

Finally, as the sun began to peek through the window and the rest of the kids began to get up, she crawled out of bed. I immediately began to tell her my ear was hurting, and I could hear whatever it was still moving. She told me to put my head in her lap so she could look at it. She grabbed my earlobe and pulled it from side to side and said she could not see anything, then abruptly stood up, letting my head fall into the seat.

After hours of complaining throughout the day, she gave in and decided to take another look. She grabbed a bottle of hydrogen peroxide and pulled out a bobby pin from her hair. She poured the peroxide into the cap and then into my ear. I could hear it bubbling inside of my ear and could feel the bug flipping around in my ear canal. She poked the bent end of the bobby pin deep into my ear canal to try and dig it out. It felt like she was punching right through my eardrum as she held my head down in her lap. "I can't see anything," she said, and told me that it had probably crawled out on its own. "But, I can still hear it," I said as she walked away, handing me a rag to hold over my ear to catch the fluid that streamed out of my ear and down my neck.

Hours had gone by listening to this bug inside my ear until it finally stopped moving. I can only assume it died or maybe even drowned in the peroxide. The pain was so bad it took everything inside of me to try to ignore it.

A few days later, one of my teachers noticed something just inside my ear. It was a body part of a cockroach. I was right. It was a cockroach! I told her the entire story as she looked inside my ear to see if she could see anything else. Later, she sent me to the school nurse who extracted the remains of the bug using a suction device. The nurse was disturbed by the story as well, along with the methods mom had used to treat it. But mostly, she was concerned about the fact that mom had stuck a bobby pin inside my ear to the point of hurting me.

Thankfully, according to the nurse my eardrum wasn't punctured, but I did begin to have ear infections quite often after that. From that night on, I covered my ears when I slept.

With all of that, it wasn't the worst place we ever lived. The furnishings, bugs, mice, and rats would be the least of my worries in the months ahead. Shortly after living in this house, we moved to another house far from my grandparents. The new place could only be described as evil!

chapter five

House of Evil Deeds

My dad took a job as a semi-truck driver for a cement
company that was many miles away from my grandparents and
the rest of my mom's family. Dad had rented an old asphalt-sided
house on a graveled and dirt road outside of the small town of
Westfield, Indiana. From the moment I entered this place, a feeling
of dread overwhelmed me. From top to bottom, from the rooms
upstairs to the closed-in back porch, it felt dark in every place I
walked through.

It sat on an acre (or so) of land that had an outhouse on the
back corner of the lot by a field. A small, wooded area separated
the house we rented from the landlord who owned most of the
property along the dirt road.

His family members lived in a beautiful farmhouse on the opposite side of the road, and they worked the fields and tended to the horses they would ride. Their son and daughter would ride their bicycles from their house to their grandparents, our landlord. We rode the same school bus and became somewhat friends. We would play with them outside of their house, and they rode their bikes down to our yard to play. But, their parents told them they were not allowed to come inside our house.

My brother built what he called "the fort" in the small, wooded area.

It was a structure of fallen tree limbs, sticks, and other objects he would find around the yard. He nailed all of the sticks and limbs together to form the walls of the fort. He threw an old tarp over the top and furnished it with an old metal chair frame. He found a piece of scrap wood to use as the seat. When we moved the chair to another area, we would hold the seat and drag the frame behind us.

It was a gathering spot for us to play, but it was his place to hide his treasures. He found value in some of the simplest things he would find. Marbles, guitar picks, and other things—but, he mostly collected money!

He dug holes to hide the mason jars of loose change that people had dropped onto the sidewalks and inside stores. He would steal coins from my dad's pant pockets that would lie on the floor at night when he slept. It was a perfect opportunity to take the change in between the snores of a sleeping dad.

We had a small, rickety wooden detached one-car garage located just outside the back door of the house. We were told not to play there because this was where my dad kept all of his tools. He would work on vehicles for the family and do welding projects for people in the area. I would see boxes and boxes of welding rods sitting under his workbench.

One evening while we were sleeping, my mom went into labor, and my aunt had driven several miles to babysit while mom and dad went to the local hospital. The following morning, our aunt began yelling at the foot of the stairs for the kids to get up and get ready for school. It took us by surprise that she was there and mom and dad had gone to the hospital. By the time we came home from school, we were greeted by dad telling us we had a new baby brother.

My aunt, having young kids of her own, would have to leave to get back to her own family, leaving our dad to care for us while mom was at the hospital. After a bean and cornbread meal and doing dishes with my oldest sister, I walked out the back door looking for my sister Donna to see if she wanted to play jump rope with me, but she was nowhere to be found.

I heard tools shuffling inside the garage where dad was working. He noticed me near the back porch and asked me to come inside the building to help him hold something while working on it. I had often helped my dad work on TVs, radios, and smaller items and would hand him tools. He always worked on something that he had salvaged.

I was intrigued as I entered the building, and was curious about what he wanted me to help him with. As I walked in his direction, he shoved over a stack of tools clearing off a section of the workbench. He then reached down and lifted me up and sat me down on the bench right in front of him. It was there at only six years old when I was sexually molested by my dad for the first time.

"I remember the garage, the bench, what I was wearing, every little detail!"

He removed my panties out from under the little blue dress my grandmother had made me, spit on his little finger, and inserted it into my body.

Oh, the pain I felt and the burning inside of me as I began to tremble. I was so scared! He told me to be quiet so that no one would come in and see what he was doing. He told me to sit still, and it would hurt for only a little while. The entire time I did not look at the face of the man I called dad, and only caught a small glance at the organ he had taken out of the front of his pants and was holding. I thought, "What is going on here?" I did not want to feel this pain or be so afraid. What is he doing to me? I had no idea what was happening, but I knew it was not good. I did not know the depths of the dark and lonely road that this experience would lead me down.

I just wanted to help my dad work on his project. I kept looking towards the house and hoping that the screen door would open. I hoped one of the other kids would walk in and see what was going on, but there was no one around. Were they playing in the fort? I did not know. I knew in my heart this was wrong, and I was so confused at what was taking place. I did not CRY or dare to SAY a word, because I was just too scared.

Suddenly we both heard the front screen door slam as my sister Donna came out yelling my name. What had seemed to last for eternity was over in a few minutes as he quickly picked me up from the workbench, sat me down on the ground handing me my panties then told me to put them back on. He began to instruct me that if I ever told anyone, he would whip me and threatened to kill me and my entire family if I did speak out.

He made threats to me about being forced to go to a foster home. I did not know what a foster home was, but he made it sound like it was a very bad place to be. He tried to justify what he had just done to me by saying that I was his favorite. His favorite? What the heck does he mean I am his favorite? He had just hurt me and threatened harm to me and my family if I said anything about what had taken place. Being a kid, it just didn't make sense to me and I had no idea how I was supposed to deal with everything that had just happened.

I felt as if the entire family's well-being had been placed on my shoulders that day. Me! A young shy little girl was now forced to protect the very family I loved. As he spoke, I began to form pictures in my mind that portrayed what a foster home might be like, and how I would never see my family again and it scared me.

Visions were filling my head of what he might do to hurt my mom and our family. They were violent and dark pictures that would never become bright again. The love I had for my dad was changed forever. He would never be the same to me from that moment on.

I quickly put my panties back on under my dress. The little blue dress that had given me such great memories with my grandma was now changed and destroyed forever.

I ran to the fort in the woods to think about and process what had just taken place.

It's where I found some of the other kids playing, including Donna. As the burning and pain continued, I later felt a wetness in my underwear. As I walked away from everyone, I wondered what was going on. I raised the front of my dress and discovered there was some blood in my panties. I began to wonder why I was bleeding.

Is it because of what he did to me? Am I cut inside? What was making me bleed and hurt so bad? I was so terrified someone would see it! How would I explain it? I did not know what to do so I simply went to the outhouse and threw them away to hide what had taken place in the garage. It was the only thing I could come up with to conceal what happened.

I made my way to the house entering the back porch, stopping at a basket filled with laundry, clean or dirty, I didn't care. At this point, I just wanted to find another pair of panties to put on.

As evening fell, I began making bottles for the toddlers and helped do the dishes. We all began to settle into our usual spots on a mattress upstairs for the night. I remember laying there, in the darkness clutching at my private area to comfort the pain that was left behind. I was so tempted to tell my older sister, but I was too afraid of what my dad might do. I decided at that moment in time, I would keep it a secret forever to protect my family.

Morning came, and with it another school day. The pain had diminished during the overnight hours, but the soreness was a stark reminder of what had happened the day before. However, it was as if the pain had moved into my heart, a kind of pain that would never go away. Along with that came a sense of loneliness, and a new identity had taken over my entire being while I was sleeping. One that became withdrawn from the world I knew before.

I didn't want to get out of bed. I felt so alone, and I most certainly did not want to go to school! I felt ashamed and tarnished. But with my mom at the hospital, I didn't want to stay home all day with my dad, either. Going to school was an escape from my dad. He became someone I feared.

I began to shuffle through some of the clothes that were on the bedroom floor and found a wrinkled up dress to put on over my underclothes and went downstairs to look for my shoes.

After putting on my shoes, I went into the kitchen to make a bottle for my little brother before the bus came. Suddenly, my dad looked at me and asked me if I felt ok or if I was sick. He began to imply that I was sick and that I needed to stay home. I had experienced a horrible trauma the day before, but I didn't have a fever or feel ill in any way. The iIllnesses and diseases I had experienced which caused a fever, is how I viewed being sick. He implied I needed to stay home, but I wanted to be as far away from him as I possibly could!

He began baiting me by saying I would be the first one to see the new baby when my mom came home that afternoon. I had been trying to process all of the stuff that went on the day before, and seeing the new baby was something that got my attention. He shuffled the other kids out of the house to catch the bus putting his hand on my shoulder holding me back as they ran towards the road.

The door on the bus was barely shut as it drove off when he dropped his pants to the floor right in front of me. I was astonished! It was the first time I ever saw a grown man's private area fully exposed! I don't know what he had in mind, but I felt extremely threatened and did not know what to expect as my heart began to pound inside my chest. I was terrified!

Who is this man I called dad, and what is he doing? What has he become? He laid me down on the bed as he began touching me and inserting his finger inside me again while caressing himself and telling me to watch the things he was doing. I did not want to look at that, and I didn't.

The older kids were gone, and I was defenseless and being held captive without hope. I felt so helpless.

My mom is going to be coming home with a new baby soon. In my mind, all of this will all go away when she gets here! Maybe she would walk in right now and catch him doing this to me. But, she did not come through the door, and oh how I wished she had.

Once he achieved his purpose, he exited the house to go work on the truck he had in the garage. He instructed me to watch the little ones and come and get him if I needed him. So, there I sat with a warm cup of coffee of my own he had given me, watching tv on an old, dial-type TV with an antenna that didn't offer much entertainment for kids to watch other than a soap opera. I was dealing with another round of what just happened as I looked at the TV, but the sights and sounds did not resonate because of the many thoughts that were going through my mind.

An hour or two had gone by, and he came in to check on us. He began to tell me how pretty I was, and that's why he liked touching me. He went on to say to me it would only hurt until I got used to it. "UNTIL I GET USED TO IT?" What the heck did he mean until I got used to it? I explained to him he had made me bleed, and I didn't want him to touch me like that anymore.

I began asking him why he was doing that stuff to himself? He simply replied that it felt good. He told me to quit asking questions and stop complaining because mom was on her way home. He reminded me I better not say anything to her or anyone else about what he had done to me during her absence. Would it hurt the other little girls in the family? With that in my mind, most of my pain turned to fear! Fear for my little sisters!

Shortly after that, my aunt drove into the driveway with my mom holding the new baby in the front seat. As sad as I was, this little boy was a bright ray of sunshine in what had begun as a dark day. I ran out to see my mom and this tiny baby, and I was going to be the first kid to hold him. Little things like this were so important to me. They made me feel special. I told her how excited I was to have her home, and hoped she would never have to go away again.

The others came home from school as we all welcomed him to the family. The excitement of the new baby soon wore off as he cried throughout the night and I took a turn to change his diaper and feed him.

An irritation began to develop in my private area. After a few days, it began to burn when I would pee. I followed my mom to the outhouse, asking her why does my pee-pee hurt so bad? She said she would look at me when she was finished to see if something was wrong.

She asked me when it started to bother me. I told her it began while she was in the hospital, but dared not say what I thought had caused the pain. I wanted to be honest with her so badly, but I was too afraid.

She instructed me to remove my panties to inspect me. She began to scold me, and accused me of touching myself and that I had dried blood in my vagina. I tried to explain that I didn't do anything to cause this, but I didn't know how to defend myself without telling her what my dad had done. I simply said with a mild quiver in my voice, I did not know why blood was there, and it just started to hurt. Her response was to keep my hands to myself, go inside the house, grab a rag, and wash off the now dried blood.

I didn't understand why she was scolding me. Her solution was to keep my hands to myself. I didn't do anything to cause this. This was not the answer I had expected. I thought she would suspect what went on while she was gone without me having to give her specific details. But, I didn't know if she had noticed anything odd when she looked at me. It was my way of giving her a sign that things happened that should not have. It was a simple way in a child's world to express something that was going on and that it hurt. She didn't seem to care and I was so heartbroken and disappointed.

I went about my usual way of being a kid, which meant that I helped take care of my siblings. Now, I had another job: to keep a secret in order to protect my family from being harmed by my dad. I think my mom knew what was going on. I overheard a conversation in which she asked my dad what was going on with me while she was gone. I heard him tell her he didn't know what she was talking about and made no claim in knowing I had issues. She never treated me the same after that. The explanation my dad gave her must have been enough for her, because nothing got better. The fact of the matter was, over time they got worse. He began forcing me to perform adult sexual acts on him without intercourse. Anytime he could get me alone and away from the rest of the family, he would seize the opportunity.

When attending school, I felt it seemed as though everyone was staring at me. Did they know what was going on at home? I couldn't force myself to make eye contact with anybody, including my teachers and the kids. I even felt different at home with my siblings. Now, I had to keep my dad from harming them.

When everyone was asleep with their dreams, mine were being torn away.

He would seek me out in every corner of the house I tried to hide. Under the piles of dirty clothes, beneath the stairway closet, everywhere I tried to hide. But for ME, there was nowhere to hide and get away from this torture. The abuse continued to happen for the next few years in this evil house.

Taking care of the younger kids gave me an outlet to keep my mind occupied with what became the perverse way of life I was forced to live. While living in Westfield, we gained a set of twins and another baby. Our family of 11 kids was outgrowing this house. With all that was going on with me and my struggles, suddenly, two of my siblings were facing battles of their own. But, they were fighting for their lives!

chapter six

Aspirin Doesn't Kill the Pain

Mom suffered a lifetime of headaches. She continually bought big bottles of 500 Bayer aspirin tablets to ease the pain. She left them on the bedside table for easy accessibility, and in that era, childproofing containers was not required. I wasn't sure if she suffered from other forms of pain, such as the multitude of pregnancies, or if they came from the physical abuse she suffered from my dad.

I remember her chewing them up all the time, and I was curious as to how they tasted. One day, I popped one into my mouth and chewed on it that caused bitter facial expressions and sounds that went along with it. I quickly ran to the sink and began spitting it out while my mom and some of the kids began laughing at me. The rusty colored well water quickly took the taste of the aspirin out of my mouth.

At this stage of growing up, the twins were fun to play with and make giggle. I didn't know that two babies could be born at the same time until mom and dad brought them home. We had newborns so often, being the youngest of the family didn't last more than a few months, and calling them "the baby" shifted from child to child.

The twins would crawl and play on piles of dirty laundry in the back of the house. It was like a playground for them as they would pull out clothes from overflowing baskets, one item at a time, while making faces and sounds to one another. Once they got to the bottom of the pile, they would put the baskets on their heads and giggle in delight as they tried to get close to one another. They would look at each through the slots of the basket with their bottles secured in between their teeth.

Soon they were well on their way to becoming curious toddlers, and what one got into, so did the other. I wasn't sure at the time who the instigator was, but I have the feeling it was my brother. I had taken great interest in both of them, but for some reason, he was my favorite.

It was routine for me to check on the twins, change their diapers and play with them after school. One afternoon when I came home from school, mom was sitting in front of the TV as she usually did with her cigarette in her hand and a cup of coffee on the table. There was an odor in the air that was familiar to me. I went to the kitchen and saw a pot of beans burning on the stove, which she must have forgotten about. I turned off the stove and told her the beans were burned.

As I walked through the house, I began looking for the twins. I made my way through the rooms calling out their names, but I wasn't getting the usual playful response. I went through the back-room doorway, searching for them. Lying there on the piles of clothes, I found both babies motionless, barely breathing with pills in their little hands and the aspirin bottle lying close by.

"I remember the house, the room, the empty bottle, every little detail!"

I yelled out for my mom with the sounds of fear in my voice with what I had just discovered. There was white foam coming from their mouths! I knelt beside my little brother and started breathing into his mouth as the taste of aspirins landed on my lips. I didn't know what I was doing, but I had been taught things at school about what to do if someone was dying and how to breathe for them. This is what I thought this was happening to my little brother. Was he dying in my arms? His little lips were so blue. His body was so limp as I watched his chest rise up and down with every one of my breaths.

I could see his twin sister was breathing ever so slightly as mom came into the room to find out what all of the commotions were about as I continued to work on him. "What the hell!" she screamed out, grabbing my sister and running towards the phone to call EMS. In between the breaths I was giving to my brother, I told her that I thought they had gotten into the bottle of aspirin!

I focused on him while my mom held my sister, looking out the front door, waiting for the ambulance to arrive. An EMS worker took control of the situation and transported them both to a local hospital. I felt powerless, and the anger I felt towards my mom at that time was so strong. But, I would not let the anger take over. Gosh, I was so mad at her! How could she have let this happen? These two babies had eaten nearly every aspirin that had been inside the bottle. All the while, my mom was watching her soap operas and burning beans on the stove. The smoking pot on the stove could have burned the house down. Now, the twins were battling to live!

They struggled for days and days to survive. I overheard mom talking to the doctor on the phone, and asking questions about brain damage. I'm sure she knew what it meant, but I didn't. The doctors diagnosed the twins as having aspirin poisoning, and weren't able to explain the effects that they might face.

I felt as if I had saved their lives by finding them when I did. Had the timing been off in the slightest, they might not have survived. How was I able to make such quick reactions to help these babies? I believe I was given the strength from within to help my siblings that day while mom was focused on the TV screen and cigarettes.

The hospital must have reported the incident to the local Child Protection Welfare Officials. Suddenly, mom began doing more of the house cleaning. Eventually, I noticed that she would only clean on the days that the social services came to check the living conditions and the kids.

This was the first time I realized that someone could take us away and put us into "foster homes." I didn't know what this meant, but it was a threat my dad had instilled in me early on. I had spent the last few years of my life trying to prevent this from happening.

After the wellness check was over, the house would go back to its typical deplorable condition. It wasn't long before the piles of clothes were scattered about, and trash was in every room. However, the new bottle of aspirin was on a shelf out of reach of the kids.

My brother had taken most of the pills and suffered a mild case of brain damage. He struggled with learning when he became old enough to go to school. He functions well as an adult, and he discovered he had talents he never knew he had while growing up. He can disassemble any kind of motor, transmission, or engine, and fix them and put them back together. So, if you ever need a good mechanic, I know a really good one.

So many bad things were happening in this little house. No amount of aspirin could erase the pain a lot of us suffered. I called it an evil place early on and hated every moment of living there. I wondered what it would take to get us out of this bad place. My dad was sexually molesting me every chance he could get and the twins had survived a terrible ordeal. **But, this house wasn't done with us yet!**

chapter seven

Highway to Hell

Dad would deliver bags of cement on pallets with a flatbed trailer for the company where he worked. He drove a beat-up old truck with only one seat, the driver's seat. One of his routes was the drive to Cincinnati, Ohio to deliver a load. The company was located along the highway just a short distance from our house, so it was convenient for his boss to have him deliver concrete with no advanced schedule—an on-call type of situation. One hot summer day, he was called to deliver a load to Cincinnati.

I was playing outside with some of the other kids wearing a little blue one-piece swimsuit. I was using the water hose to spray them down while I enjoyed watching them run around the yard. It was our form of cooling off on the hot, humid summer days.

Nothing was finer to me as a big sister than to hear their giggles and watch them be kids. They had a sense of normalcy that I felt I was missing.

As I was enjoying the moment and laughter, my dad stuck his head out of the front door. He yelled for me to come inside. I assumed I needed to do something for mom or one of the babies. I didn't know why I was being summoned. I heard him say, "get some shoes on," as I walked into the house, letting the screen door slam behind me. "Why?" I asked as I looked around the floor to find a pair of flip flops. "You are going with me to Cincinnati." Cincinnati?

I knew it was just a ploy to get me alone, and I did not want to go with him. I tried to use the excuse that I didn't know where my shoes were. My clothes are wet. Mom needs me to help her. "You are not going to need shoes," he said. As he handed me a towel to dry off, he told me to get into the car.

He drove us to the truck yard where he found an old wooden crate lying outside the office. He put the crate inside the cab of the truck for me to sit on. I covered it with the thin "Breeze" laundry soap towel that he had given me so I would not get my wet swimsuit or legs dirty. He put the truck into gear, and off we went. I began to count the numerous bridges we drove under as we headed East on the interstate. It was my first experience on a major highway, and I was excited to see where it led.

After an hour or so of driving, we stopped at this big gas

station with lots of trucks parked on the pavement. "Truck Stop" was the sign I remember reading as we pulled in. I didn't know what it was other than a place to get gas and eat.

We went inside the diner and took a seat in a booth where my bare feet dangled while waiting for the waitress to take our order. My dad ordered food for both of us and a single glass of iced tea with lemon he would share with me. I didn't like lemon in tea, but realized it was all I was going to get. He got up and said he would be right back as he made his way to the men's room.

The waitress delivered our plates with the biggest cheeseburger I had ever seen. French fries, pickles, tomatoes and all the goodies that are typical for such a meal. She asked if everything was ok. I explained I did not like the lemon tea, and I showed her that I was not wearing any shoes, but my dad **made me** come with him anyway. She said she would bring me a Coke and told me that it was ok that I wasn't wearing shoes. I tried to let her know I did not want to be alone with my dad. When I said, "made me," I looked at her in an attempt to give her a sign that she did not notice. She came back to the table, swapping out the tea with a big, ice-cold glass of coke that I had to use both hands to hold while drinking it.

After we had eaten, we left the café and went back to the truck. I jumped in and sat on the box as he walked around to get inside to drive; however, he did not put the key into the ignition to hit the road. Nope, he had other plans!

I was so short I could stand up inside of the cab of this truck!

He made me strip off the bathing suit I was wearing and stand next to him as he began to fondle my body as he proceeded to caress his genitals. I turned my head to look out of the window. I wondered if anyone would take notice of what was going on inside of this cab. Men even walked by the truck and pretended that they did not see that I was naked or acknowledge the motions my dad was going through.

I tried to make eye contact with them as they walked by so that they would "catch him in the act." I hoped that it would solve all of my problems. But, none of them would look at me! As I look back, now I know they had to have seen what was taking place. I imagine they knew and just did not want to get involved.

My dad had a reputation for having a bad temper within the local trucking industry. I wondered if this was why no one would take action. I felt as if I was invisible in a very public and highly active parking lot. Why did I have to witness what guys do to themselves in the trucks they drive. Why was I being used as a pawn for my dad's pleasure? I just wanted to be at home, spraying the kids with the water hose and playing.

Finally, after he did his thing, he handed me my bathing suit and told me to sit back down on the crate as he started the truck's engine, and we headed out of the parking lot. When we arrived at our destination, we went inside the building. A very nice young lady greeted us and even gave me a candy bar and a can of pop to enjoy. At the same time, she processed the delivery paperwork as workers unloaded the pallets to the dock.

As we departed the docks and headed West, the sun began to set, creating a bright glare on the dirty windshield. Through the rays of sunlight, I could see the truck stop and the very spot we had parked just hours earlier. As we drove by on the divided highway and with traffic flying by, I recalled every moment about the trauma that had taken place there and I was glad we did not stop.

When we arrived home and walked inside, we saw my mom watching TV and kids sleeping throughout the house. It was as though nothing had happened. I made my way to the kitchen and turned on the light to find any leftovers I could eat. All I saw was the massive pile of dishes in the sink with cockroaches running all over them, trying to gather up the crumbs left behind. It didn't matter if I ate or not. I was mentally exhausted and went to bed hungry once more.

I thought about the waitress and the lady who gave me candy and a can of pop—how they both had been so lovely and made me feel so special. I reflected on those moments as I made my way up to the room with no walls and mentally relived the day. *I was talking to people with my eyes, but they were not listening.* As I laid there and as hard as I tried to focus on other things like the kids' laughter earlier in the day, the same bad visions kept coming into my head.

"I remember the diner, the truck, my bathing suit, every little detail!"

chapter eight

Shop With a Cop

Many local charities gave us things like food, school supplies, and recycled clothing. One morning, I was sitting in my classroom around Christmas time when I heard my name called over the intercom speakers, along with the names of my siblings. I began to think we were being taken out of the school because we might be sent home or something. Instead, school officials met us and paired each one of us up with police officers. They were taking us to shop in a nearby town for the annual "Shop With A Cop" charity event. We were going to shop at The Mall! My first time ever!

As we approached the building, I saw the beautiful winter wonderland scenes in the big picture windows; all decked out for the holiday season. I could hardly wait to go inside! We were escorted in with our police officer, who had driven us to begin our wondrous shopping adventure. There were also kids from other schools in the stores, and each of them had an officer helping them pick out items.

Inside one of the many stores, a young sales lady greeted me with lots of enthusiasm. She had shoulder-length blond hair and was wearing a headband that matched her outfit, which I thought was so pretty. She took my hand and led me to a rack of 6x size clothes, my size. My host police officer looked as if he knew how to shop for a little girl, but I felt the lady knew more how to please a little girl and knew what she was doing more than he did.

She asked me questions about my favorite colors. "Pink. I like pink," I told her as we walked through the different types of clothing. I picked out a pink dress with pinstripes. It had a wide collar around the scoop neckline and a black patent leather belt. I also picked out a matching pair of shoes, and socks that were topped with a lace ribbon. They were so cute to a kid who never got to pick out new items, and this was such a thrill. The officer paid for the dress, shoes, underwear, socks, a slip, and a headband, which they took the tag off so I was able to wear immediately. I wanted a headband because my sales lady was wearing one, and it made me feel like a princess.

Respect and great memories were made that day that will last a lifetime!

"I remember the shoes, the dress, the officer, every little detail!"

I was excited about getting new clothes. My oldest sister was embarrassed as we carried our bags into school just long enough to board the bus and go home. As we took our seats holding our bags of goodies, the kids laughed at us for getting the "Welfare Clothes."

My oldest sister just hated it and said she would not wear any of them. She cried as we got off the bus and, in her anger, threw her bags down in the driveway. I tried to make her feel better and picked them up, telling her the clothes were beautiful as she stomped into the house, tossing her schoolbooks to the floor.

I walked in proudly with my stuff and especially the new dress and took it out of the bag to show it off. I wanted to wear it the next day to school, so I hung it on a nail located right above the baby's bed to keep it looking nice and new.

While we were at school, the sink would become full of dirty dishes—the coffee cups from my mom and dad, along with a multitude of sour-smelling baby bottles. Anything and everything used during the day while we were at school had to be cleaned.

My older sister would help with them right before we were supposed to go to bed. She always complained about washing tons of silverware. She would put it in the bottom of the sink to soak. There was always so much of it. It took so long to wash just the silverware before she could start the pots and pans, a sure sign we were getting close to being done. On one occasion, she was swirling the dish rag inside a drinking glass when the top broke off and cut her hand. She looked at me and said, "It looks like you have to finish them now. "She was right. She wrapped her hand in a towel to stop the bleeding and watched TV with the rest of the family.

The next morning, I woke up excited to wear my new dress, shoes, and headband to school. I discovered that the baby had pulled the brand-new dress off the nail and peed all over it. It was so nasty I could not wear it! I was devastated and disappointed that the dress I was so proud of and dreamt about wearing was an ugly mess.

I had to find something to wear before the bus got there. I found a shirt and a pair of pants, slipping on my new shoes and the headband around my head, and ran out the door to get on the bus. The kids at school did not hold back the whistles. They called us dogs, bullied, and laughed at us. They asked me if this was the clothes the officers bought me. "It looks like you got those clothes out of the trash," I remember one of them saying.

There was no reason to tell them how the new dress was ruined overnight by my baby brother. The harassment from the kids went on all day. I honestly do not remember a single teacher or anyone in authority stopping these kids from treating me with this kind of humiliation. I just went about my day because there were far more important things going on at home that they could never begin to understand nor were they aware of. I had to keep my secrets from all of them, including the officer that took me shopping the day before.

I would have to become a much braver person to not reveal all of those horrible secrets. This experience would be just one step of my journey to become stronger in the days, weeks, and even in the years to come.

chapter nine

The Great Escape

There was no guidance in our household or the homes of most of my extended families. We all just lived in the same type of houses with adults. We were not taught the basic elements of day to day life. The only value I felt I had in my family was to be another name on the list of kids we had on the food stamp application. That, and helping with my siblings, of course.

My older sister was the epitome of the first child syndrome. She was spoiled and was allowed to do things with her group of friends. She had taken an interest in an older guy and started to date at an incredibly early age. On weekends, she was permitted to go on overnight trips to his grandmother's house, as long as one of the other kids went with her—a chaperone, of sorts. This is the kind of family I grew up in—no boundaries, guidance, or respect for any aspect of life.

The one who was selected to go, was to keep an eye on them to not sneak off into a room alone. Yeah, right! Put a kid in front of a *color* TV with a cartoon and they will be distracted for hours.

After she came home from the overnight visits, I could overhear some of my sister's conversations on the phone with her girlfriends from school. She would talk and brag about having sex. When I began to eavesdrop on her conversations, I didn't know what she was describing was called SEX. She would go away overnight, come home, and have constant phone conversations about what she did with her boyfriend.

I never got to go, and I didn't know what they were doing or even cared. It is the first time I can recall hearing the term "having sex." I was a naive kid, and I wasn't sure what it entailed. Little did I know, some of the things my dad was doing to me was in the same category.

One weekend, several of the kids argued whose turn it was to go with her. My older brother won the battle that weekend and I was to keep an eye on the fort. They piled into her boyfriend's car, and off they went with the radio blasting to rock and roll music. As they headed out of the driveway, spinning the tires on the gravel and dirt road, I waved my hand to clear the dust from my face as the cloud curled behind them as they made their way to the paved highway.

A few minutes later, dad and my little sister, Cathy, left with a few empty metal fuel cans. Fall was setting in, and dad would make trips to fill them for the space heater. They hadn't been gone for more than an hour when they came back home, and dad came storming through the front door in a state of panic! He began yelling at my mom, "The kids were in a wreck on the highway!" The kids are being taken to the hospital. We all were startled and feared the worst.

Dad had recognized the crushed and mangled vehicle my siblings were riding in while on his route to get the fuel. They had rear-ended a parked flatbed semi-trailer that had not pulled off the highway, leaving a portion of the trailer sticking out into the traffic lane.

Dad was told by the first responders they were taking all three of them to Methodist hospital in Indianapolis. They explained that one of them was critical, and was in a life or death situation. What the hell? Didn't we just go through something like this?

Mom began searching for her pocketbook in a state of panic. She told me to watch the kids and to call my aunt in the neighboring town of Kokomo. Mom wanted my aunt to come to our house and help me with the rest of the kids. I called her and told her what was going on. My aunt explained it would take her about an hour to get here.

The cold had settled in as I added wood to the potbelly stove to keep us warm as the sun began to set while waiting for my aunt.

The same stove that had burned my back on a few occasions from my dad's abuse was now offering a sense of comfort for the kids. At ten years old, I was now in charge of the household!

Before my aunt arrived, the phone rang. On the other end of the line was a person asking for permission to operate on my brother. I explained my mom and dad were on their way to the hospital, and my aunt was coming from Kokomo. He asked to talk to an adult. I was scared by the sound of the urgency he had in his voice, and at the time, I knew this was important. He said they needed to operate on my brother, or he would die. I lied to him, telling him my aunt was coming in the door right now and to hold on while I handed her the phone. I took a deep breath, lowered the tone in my voice, and said hello. The man identified himself as a doctor, said he needed to perform surgery right now and wanted permission to do so.

I felt as if GOD had given me the courage to talk and gave me an adult voice to permit him to do the surgery. He hung up on me as soon as I said yes. As I hung up the phone, I began to worry and wonder if I would ever see my brother again. I asked myself if I would ever hang out in the fort or watch him pick that old plastic guitar. I had a sense of loneliness and felt so badly for him. But, I had to get the kids settled in and be the grown-up until my aunt got there to spend the rest of the night with us.

The following morning, my aunt had to leave and I was left alone with the younger kids until mom and dad came home from the hospital. Mom and dad were making several trips back and forth during the most critical days to be with my brother. With all the commotion of the accident going on, we all missed a day or so of school. That prompted a wellness check from the school officials. The local police knew about the accident, so an officer and a social service woman came to the house while my mom and dad were at the hospital.

They toured the house, asking me questions I could not answer, and told me to have mom or dad call them when they got home. They had been making periodic visits to the house since the aspirin incident. Still, this visit was spontaneous. The true story about the living conditions of the house was now exposed. They saw how unfit this house really was and how it was not being cleaned regularly. It was not suitable for a family, especially with crawling babies. Cockroaches, rats, and mice were tenants that lived among us, and it was the normal way of life of our family.

My oldest sister came home from the hospital a few days later with her knee stitched up and a broken heart. She felt responsible for the condition of what her brother was enduring and fighting for his life. She told us stories of the horrific views she had seen of our brother's head. His forehead had been crushed, revealing scattered grey matter mixed with glass from the windshield. We all just wanted our brother to get well, but this was going to be a long road. He would not be coming home anytime soon.

One evening in the dark of the night, mom and dad came to

every room in the house, waking us up, telling us to get dressed and then loaded us into our station wagon with whatever we could fit between the kids and the seats. I sat in the back by the rear window with some of the kids who were still in diapers. It was a road trip that seemed to take hours. A real true story of over the river and through the woods to grandma's house we'd go.

As the miles went on, the kids began to settle in from the excitement of being woken up in the middle of the night. They went back to sleep, leaning on each other. We drove under clear skies and the light of the moon as we approached Peru, Indiana. Suddenly the sky lit up with the brightest falling star and a tail like no other! The glow reflected the entire inside of the car and lit up the nearby woods as it streaked across the sky. It was a fantastic sight to see.

"I remember the night, the car, the falling star, every little detail!"

Was this a sign of a dramatic change that was about to happen in our family? Was a life failing? Were we losing my brother? I feared my brother's fight was over, and my mom and dad did not want to tell us. Why were we leaving in the middle of the night to go to grandma's house miles and miles away?

We finally arrived at my grandparents' house in Northern Indiana with nothing more than what the car could hold. We carried sleeping kids into the house, laying them on blankets my grandmother had put down on the floor. I cuddled up with the little twin brother as I watched the flickering flames of the gas stove in their living room.

I was listening to mom tell my grandparents about our brother, who was making progress. This was a last-ditch effort to avoid the local children's services in Westfield. They were planning on removing the children from my mom and dad because of the deplorable conditions we lived in. We had fled the county to get away before the local child welfare officials could take all of us to foster homes. We had made a great escape in the dark of night!

chapter ten

House Hopping

While my mom and dad were searching for a place to live, all ten kids had been divided between the homes of grandparents, aunts, and uncles. Dad had found a place to rent rather quickly. We were amazed to find ourselves in a beautiful country home in Miami County shortly after we fled Westfield.

During move-in day, I kept the kids entertained. The adults began to bring in the roach filled sofa, the TV, the refrigerator, and one of the bed bugged mattresses, which they leaned against the living room wall. All of the nasty stuff we left behind was being moved in bit by bit.

There were boxes of dishes, pots and pans, and any food we had was put in the kitchen to unpack. Piles of clean and dirty clothes were brought inside in baskets and boxes. It didn't matter if they were clean or dirty—they were just thrown into a room to be sorted out later.

This house was unlike we had ever lived in before! It had amazing hardwood floors. An oak staircase spiraled up from the living area that led to several bedrooms. A huge yard with several trees filled the lawn with autumn leaves that gave us a place to play while the move was taking place. We made a huge pile of leaves to dive into. It was all fun and games until Donna and I came down with a massive case of hives. Our faces were swollen with welts running into each other. Our eyes were nearly swollen shut, and our lips were puffed out like we were wearing the wax candy lips.

The following morning our grandma came over to help with the move. As she always did, she jumped right in and started cooking. She dug out a bag of government white rice while my mom began unpacking boxes that held our dishes.

The water pump for the well had issues, and grandma needed water for cooking. She found a few jugs in all the mess, and told Donna and I to go down to the neighbor's house to get some water. It was down the road, about ¼ of a mile away from us. We laughed about how ugly we were the day before with the case of hives we had from playing in the falling leaves as we made our way to the house.

We walked up to the door, knocked, and waited for the door to open. As the door opened, there stood a woman drying her hands on the apron she was wearing. She said hello and asked us what we needed. I told her our grandma sent us here to get water as we held up the empty jugs explaining the water was not working at our new house.

She took the jugs and walked towards her kitchen as Donna and I stood at the door, patiently waiting. She asked us about how many kids we had in the family. We looked down at our fingers and counted off the names of the kids, from the oldest to the youngest. "Oh yeah, my mom might be having another baby too," I added as she handed us the filled containers of water.

Her husband entered the room because he had overheard the conversations that we were having with his wife. He told us to have our dad call him about the pump for the well and what could be done to fix the water issues. I told him I would tell him to call them when he came back home. We took the filled jugs and began our long walk back to the house.

As we struggled with the heavy jugs of water, Donna and I spoke about how that lady was so nosy. Donna wondered why she asked so many questions about us as she stopped in the middle of the road to set down the heavy jugs of water to rest her arms.

I began to worry if we should have talked about all of the kids with the neighbors and said, "Donna, I think we are going to get into trouble and we need to get back home."

"Why are we going to get into trouble? she asked, wondering what we had done as we made our way back to the house.

"I think these people are the landlords of the house," I said to her as we approached the porch. I told her to not say anything about the questioning that took place.

How could we have known they were the owners of the house that we were moving into? The landlord could see all the kids in the yard, and the kind of stuff was being moved inside of this beautiful home. I could only imagine what they thought as they discovered how many kids we had and what kind of furniture we brought with us.

The move was still in progress as we lugged the jugs of water into the kitchen. Our grandmother added the water needed to make the rice. She later added butter and sugar to it as it cooked to a tender dish, which was more like a dessert. Then, she scooped it into bowls that mom had unpacked.

The younger kids sat on the kitchen floor with their legs spread apart, and I began digging out spoons from the box marked "silverware" while we were waiting for the bowls of rice to cool.

Dad entered the house all worn out from moving when the phone rang. Mom answered it and said, "Who is this?" Then, she replied with, "Oh, ok, he's right here," she said as she handed the phone to my dad, telling him it was the landlord. Knowing the facial expressions of my dad, I knew he was about to lose it. I heard him reply "ok" to the person on the other end of the line as he began to curse about the money he had given him and that he would need the money back in order to find another place to live.

He slammed down the phone and began to rage at my mom, trying to find out who had told them how many family members were living in the house. Donna and I looked at each other, knowing it was us who had spilled the beans. We were so afraid of getting beaten for telling them how many people we had in our family—she ran upstairs to get out of the way.

Dad started kicking boxes and yelling at mom as I gathered up the babies from the floor to take them upstairs to keep them out of the way.

My grandmother yelled at my dad. You should have told them how many kids you have and explained to him that it wasn't our fault for telling him. Grandma grabbed her purse and left while our mom and dad continued to fight.

They were kicking us out before we had even unpacked. We moved so often in a single year. I had gone to three different elementary schools during my third grade, and we had not even been enrolled in the new school yet. I poked my head down the edge of the stairway during the screaming match and was seen and told to get myself into bed. "What bed?" I wondered. The kid's mattresses had not been moved yet!

The little ones were crying as the arguments went on well into the night. I laid on the floor with nothing but a jacket to cover my body, wondering where we were going to live next as I finally drifted off to sleep.

A few days later we landed in a tiny little house in Macy,

Indiana while waiting for my brother to get well enough to come home from the hospital. When he did, he was not the same person who had gotten into that car to be the chaperone. He had a dent in the middle of his forehead and had lost some memories. I spent many hours teaching him about the life he had before the accident.

I told him about the fort in the woods, the secret treasures he had buried, and the landlord's freezer we used to rob all the time. I also described the plastic guitar he used to play that he could not recall.

The center section of his forehead had been crushed, which caused a dent to form in between his eyebrows. Another surgery had to be scheduled in order to protect his head. The doctors needed to insert a plastic plate to replace the missing skull that was once his forehead. Meanwhile, in order to protect his head, it was wrapped in gauze and tape for a very long time. It was a difficult time for him. I did my best and kept the little ones away from him. So, I protected him. He and I worked together to help him remember the names of his siblings. I assisted him in doing some of the more simple things that we take for granted.

Unlike the cold and darkness of our last house, this house became a healing place for my brother and a place where I felt somewhat comfortable. With all of this activity, I got a break from my dad, who was busy with moving. I am sure he did not have the time or desire to risk molesting me. There were no places to hide here for him to molest me nor was there a place for me to hide from him.

One of the advantages of moving here was the school was located practically in our backyard. There was a playground we could play at after school. The accident and all of the moving caused stress on the family—we all just wanted a place to call home. Would this be the house where we stayed? I hoped not, because there was not enough space for this many kids to live in.

chapter eleven

A Thief Among Us

Old small-town schools were built to maximize space with one doorway to enter and to exit. Huge windows would allow the bright sunlight in and keep the cost of electricity down while circulating the air by tilting out the bottom windowpane with the attached rod.

There were built-in bookcases in the back of the room, which were sectioned out into cubicles for the kids to put their personal items in, such as lunch sacks, writing paper, pencil boxes, and gym clothes. Each one had a name tag to identify the compartment we claimed. The short kids took the bottom levels, and the taller kids took the upper.

There were shared coat rooms in between the classrooms.

Students in one class used hooks on their side to hang jackets on, while kids in the other class used the opposite side. My sister and brother were in the same grade level, so they were in the same classroom. However, they had to have their desks separated because my brother liked to antagonize my sister. I was in the adjoining room, so we shared the same coatroom and saw each other often.

In the warmer months, we had recess outside. There was a small playground with rusty equipment like a jungle gym, teeter-totters, and swings that could get high enough you could look inside the windows of the building. It would take a lot of effort to get short legs to move fast enough to get that high, so I didn't even bother trying. I was satisfied with pushing my sister on the swing and watching the other kids play as I waited for the bell to ring for us to come back inside. It was my favorite place just to sit and think. I remember wishing that I could be as happy as the rest of the kids on the playground.

On rainy days and colder months, we hung our jackets in the coatroom and it was where kids would change into their gym shoes to play inside the gymnasium. My siblings and I barely had street shoes that were decent enough to wear to school, let alone having a pair of gym shoes to wear once a day at school. It was the year I was given the most beautiful red wool coat with big black buttons on it. While others saw it as a 'hand me down' I felt the value in it when I wore it because it made me feel special and so pretty.

Games like basketball and dodgeball were a popular form of

getting exercise on the main floor. For girls, it was jump rope on the sidelines. Kids without proper footwear were not allowed onto the gym floor. They were not able to participate in most of those activities.

Even as badly as my brother wanted to play, he was not allowed to join in. The likelihood of the damage he would cause to the highly polished floor with his street shoes was just not permitted. The teacher in charge would yell at him to get off the floor time and time again as he would sneak out and try to blend in with the other kids trying not to get caught. He did it every time until they eventually made him sit on a bleacher until lunchtime.

During the lunch period, my sister Donna, my little brother, and I went to the coatroom to grab our jackets to begin the short walk across the parking lot to go home. The others continued to play until they headed to the cafeteria to eat their lunches.

The three of us were inside the coat room when my brother spotted a pair of penny loafers with two shiny dimes in them. Oh, how badly I wanted to have coins in my loafers, but I would never have considered taking them. I couldn't bring myself to do that. While I saw how pretty it made the shoes, my brother only saw the money. He picked up the shoes and began taking the dimes out. I told him that he was stealing and that he would get into trouble, but he didn't care. I took my coat and left the coatroom so I would not be there if a teacher were to walk in.

Instead of going home, he wanted to walk in the opposite

direction towards the local town store. Since I was the older sister and the responsible one, I couldn't leave them alone. So, I followed behind both of them as we approached the store entrance. I stood outside under the awning, because I knew that this was something I didn't want to be a part of. He and my sister came out with a few pieces of penny candy and grape-flavored gumballs, one of my favorites. They were the real deep purple balls with the crunchy outer layer. When he offered me a piece, I was not able to turn it down. We all know what GRAPE colored anything does to your mouth and tongue.

I didn't steal the dimes, and I didn't buy the gum. Therefore, I knew I was not a thief. That was how I justified taking the gum out of the wrapper and popping it into my mouth. The intense flavor of the grape began to make my mouth water. It began to turn my tongue purple.

We had skipped lunch and headed back to school. Our mouths were as purple as purple could be as we walked back towards the school, laughing and sticking out our tongues at each other, taking our time to get back to class. Gum was not allowed at school, so we all spit it out on the sidewalk as we entered the building.

As soon as we walked into the coatroom, we were called "a pack of thieves" by the kids, including the shoes' owner with the now-empty slots. There was no way any of us could deny it. We were caught red-handed! Here we stood, with purple mouths and my brother and sister with hidden candy in the pockets of their coats. I had not taken or bought anything, and I didn't have anything in my possession. Poor kids and candy just did not go hand in hand, so we became the primary suspects!

Three different teachers interrogated us separately. When I was asked if I knew who took the dimes, I just could not lie. I defended myself and my sister, telling them it was my brother, throwing him under the bus. I was not going to take the fall for his actions and be titled a thief. But, none of that mattered. I had a purple stain in my mouth, and that was all they needed to convict me as an accomplice. The teachers had us gather outside of our classroom and awaited the principal's sentencing, who was now coming down the hall with his wooden paddle in hand.

My brother was the first to bend over, grab his ankles as Donna and I watched and waited for our turn. Whack, whack, whack, the sounds echoed down the hall. After which, the principal directed him to return to the classroom as the tears began to stream down his face. I watched as Donna took her punishment, bending over and feared my fate. She took it like a man, but I was scared to death!

I took a deep breath as I stepped towards the principal, looking up at him. He leaned down and began whispering to me that because I had confessed, he was not going to paddle me as hard, as I exhaled in relief. But, he still had to paddle me. So, in all of my bravery, I bent over to take the punishment. He only struck me once, and it didn't even hurt enough to make me cry.

He could have paddled me a thousand times over, but it would never be able to take away the shame I felt that day. We lived a life most did not understand by being so poor. Now, we would never live down the fact that my family was tagged as thieves!

So, if you happen to be wearing a pair of penny loafers and catch me looking down at them smiling, I am not looking at the color or how cute they are. I am remembering a great life lesson I carry with me still to this day, from a principal's name I wish I could recall.

chapter twelve

Fluttering Pages

One of the many third-grade schools I attended had a library
full of the most fascinating books. I remember feeling like the
books took me places that seemed to be far better than where
I was at that time in my life. That all changed when a teacher
named Mr. Crum entered my life. He was a stern teacher who did
not allow any kind of monkey business in his classroom. If kids
acted up, he would draw circles on the chalkboard and ordered
the troublemakers to stand on their tiptoes and keep their noses
inside the circle. We often had the view of some of our classmates'
backsides. Because I was shy and well-behaved, I didn't have to
suffer this indignity. Still, my brother and his friend were often at
the blackboard, standing on their tiptoes and making a spectacle of

themselves. Kids chuckled at them to the teacher's dismay as they walked up to begin their disciplinary sentence.

Mr. Crum gave us the assignment to read a book, followed by what many kids dread—giving an oral book report in front of the entire class. I found myself reading that book three or four times because I was so wrapped up in the storyline. I wanted to feel confident and proud to give the best review of the book that I could. It was an old Nancy Drew book, with the plot centering on a great mystery of secrets with a twist at every turn. It certainly held my attention. One of the first few chapters, it described the main character as being born on Christmas day, which made her a Christmas baby. I was not sure what it meant at the time, but the fast-paced drama and the story's plot kept me intrigued and glued to the pages.

My heart was pounding as Mr. Crum called my name on the day we gave our reports; even the night before, I was anxious. I handed the book to him, and he began to scan through the pages, picking out details so that he could question me.

As I began my report, I started by telling my audience, our classmates, what the book was about. My nerves had my knees trembling and the palm of my hands sweating. Right in the middle of my opening statement, Mr. Crum interrupted me and asked what kind of baby it was. I was not sure what he was asking, so I simply replied, "She was a girl baby. "He repeated the question as he elevated the tone of his voice, "What kind of baby was it?" I answered meekly, "She was a girl baby, born on Christmas Day, and her name was Abigail."

He suddenly became aggravated and angry. He began to criticize and humiliate me in front of the entire class. I could see the tension build in the other students faces as he spoke. He yelled at me, saying I had not read the book and that I was going to get an 'F.' He threw the book in my direction, and I stood there and watched the pages flutter through the air as it came towards me. The book landed at my feet with the picture of Abigail looking at me. I was crushed!

I picked up the book and made my way back to my seat in total disgrace; I was emotionally drained from what I thought would be a great day to be so ridiculed in front of my classmates. I was so disappointed in myself. How could I have forgotten one of the beginning parts of the story? I was so nervous and terrified by Mr. Crum that I had forgotten that Abigail was called a Christmas Baby. I struggled through my emotions as I sat in my seat and watched the next student be reduced to ashes in the same fashion. Nearly every student in the class couldn't wait until this unpleasant teacher would move on to another grade level or be removed from the teachers' roster. I thought the best relief would come if our family moved yet again. I started to wonder if perhaps I wasn't cut out for this 'reading thing.' It completely changed my interest in reading books for a very long time. Instead of motivating many of the other students and me, Mr. Crum was one of those teachers who criticized you no matter how hard you tried.

Even at that early age, I soon discovered that the actions, words, and behavior of a teacher could change the progression of a child's attitude and diminish their self-esteem. This can have an everlasting effect, especially on a school-age kid who comes from poverty. Sadly, I had many teachers during my elementary school years who should have been (and were supposed to be) a role model. They failed terribly in carrying out that responsibility.

It saddens me that I can only remember the names of a few teachers of mine over the years. Of those I can remember, it was their inappropriate behavior and the awful way they treated me that I remember the most. I was one of the 'stupid students' they had to deal with, and some teachers were not afraid to even say it out loud. I can vividly remember being called stupid.

My classmates were not the only ones who bullied my siblings and me. Some of the faculty also engaged in behavior that I would consider to be bullying.

Teachers had their favorites, and I was one of them in first grade with the teacher who noticed the dress my grandmother made me. All of my teachers seemed to have one or two 'pets.' But, the students like myself who didn't have the parental support, needed that one special person in our lives to help us navigate through this incredibly complex life that we were living in. We were often left behind to struggle with homework that never got done. Sadly, that cycle continues today.

CRYING WITHOUT TEARS

Of all the schools we had attended, this one had to be the worst. It was a terrible school that allowed the kids to bully my family. Coupled with all of the events that were taking place within the walls of our house just across the parking lot, the time spent here was miserable. The fights that mom and dad were having about the expenses from the many trips to Indianapolis were frequent, and some were extremely violent.

With every move we made, nobody got to know much about us. Our story was told to others by the clothing and shoes we wore. The students and teachers alike did not know how our family struggled, nor could they know about the poverty level in which we lived. We had worn out our welcome in this small community and the school. I was ready to move! Again!

chapter thirteen

Krazy Kewanna

As fate would have it, the little house in Macy was condemned and we had to move. It might have been because the owner was ready for us to leave or because of the damage done by our unruly family. Broken windows that were not replaced, wet ceilings from leaks, and the back-porch roof that had fallen in.

It was the very spot where my dad once forced me to perform a sexual act on him as kids played on the schoolyard playground. Many sad events happened here, but it was a short-lived place. With every move, distractions would keep my dad's attention on things other than molesting me. Another move would keep his mind occupied for a short time.

I tried to make a note of the few good memories that I would be able to look back on and be proud of or laugh about in the houses we lived in. In Westfield, it was saving the lives of the twins! The first house in Macy was the beautiful country home, where Donna and I looked weird as we were covered in hives from a pile of fall leaves

The memories I took with me from the house near the school in Macy gave me more shameful moments than joy. It took a while to recall a moment or a special event that I could look back on and laugh at myself or a family member. I settled on one that offered both a moment of pain and laughter from one single sibling event.

My oldest sister had pierced her ears and wore the cutest pair of post-style earrings to keep the holes she punctured open. She had done it to herself and was trying to talk Donna and I into letting her do it to us. She explained that it did not hurt much and convinced me to let her do it. Donna did not want to have anything to do with it, and left the room.

She prepared me for the procedure, which started by her giving me two ice cubes she had wrapped into cloths and told me to hold them on my ear lobes. She removed pins from the diaper of one of our siblings that she would use to punch through my ears. With a towel on the sink, a bottle of alcohol, and the huge diaper pins ready, she waited for me to get the courage to let her do the procedure. She kind of pressured me into doing it by calling me a big sissy.

I held the ice on my ears until the sting of the cold had turned my ear lobes a bright pink color. I threw what was left of the ice into the sink. Then I sat in the chair to let her pierce my ears. She quickly grabbed one of the diaper pins, dipping it into a bowl of alcohol, and began poking it through my ear. It hurt like hell as she told me to sit still as she clipped it closed. I would have been happy with just one pierced ear because of the pain, but I would be brave and sit through the next ear! With both diaper pins closed, she told me that I had to wear them for a few days. I walked around with these stupid diaper pins in my ears over the entire weekend. She could have gotten me a pair of post-style earrings but I think she took pleasure in my discomfort.

The kids and other family members teased me. I even had to laugh at myself when I looked in the mirror and saw the big diaper pins through my ears, and I was thankful I was able to hide them with my long hair.

This move could not have come at a better time for me. I had been labeled as a thief and ridiculed about the level of my reading skills. Our dad found a house in the middle of nowhere surrounded by cornfields near Kewanna. One of the benefits we received living here was that the farmers grew popcorn—a favorite snack of ours. There were a great many varieties, including white, yellow, and even purple, which looked pretty but tasted weird.

Our dad would make us walk the fields' outer rows and pick off the ears from the stocks before the farmers came in with their combines to harvest the crops. Afterward, he would force us to walk the rows to collect any ears left behind by the machinery. We shelled the kernels off the cobs into five-gallon buckets until we had blisters on our fingers. My dad was selling it to the locals in town to make a buck or two. We had such an abundance of popcorn that it was served as a food group at dinner.

My grandparents place became a hub for the family, and we would visit them often. Too often if you asked my grandpa. He had retired after working in a manufacturing plant and bought a lot in the quiet little community of Nyona Lake. There was a mobile home from the '50s on it with the promise of building a house for my grandma. He had made some progress, but it was never enough to call any single room complete.

Grandpa was content to read his TV Guide and watch the programs he had circled when they aired. He loved saltine crackers with butter on them and snacked on them often. Sometimes I would sneak one from the plate when he wasn't looking. It is likely where I had acquired the taste for "buttered crackers," as our family called them.

Conversations were held about my brother's health and well-being and proceeded to shift towards how much money our family was going to get from a lawsuit my mom and dad had filed against the trucking company.

They talked about numbers of upwards of $50, 000 and how they were planning to spend it. When the case was finalized, the attorney recommended that $30,000 of it be held in a trust fund for my brother. The rest was awarded to my mom and dad as their portion of the settlement, after the attorney took his cut.

It was here that our brother came home from the hospital for the third and final time. The doctors had put a plate inside his forehead and he would only have to go back if there were complications. When they brought him home, he was anxious to show me what his head looked like. He and I found a place to hide away from everyone else so we could gently remove the bandages so I could see what they had done to him.

At first, it was hard to look at the multitude of stitches that spanned across the top of his forehead from one ear to the other. I said whatever I could say to make him feel better about the huge scar that would be left behind. I praised him, saying the dent in the middle of his forehead was gone! "Would you look at that?" I said as he and I looked in a mirror together.

I was genuinely afraid he would get hurt as he began the final healing stage from the horrific accident he had been through. Again, I did everything I could think of to protect him and keep him safe.

He later went to school for a brief time until they felt it wasn't safe for him to be there. The multi-level building had too many dangerous factors. This made it an unsafe environment for a kid who had gone through so much trauma. He was also self-conscious about the scars left behind on his face and head. He was fine staying at home. I brought homework assignments to him to do in place of being in a classroom.

It was also the best Christmas we ever had! There were wrapped presents under the Christmas tree. This year, we were not constantly looking out the window and waiting for a charity to bring us the typically unwrapped toys and baskets of food.

Under the biggest Christmas tree I ever saw, some gifts could not be disguised by decorative wrapping paper. There was a new guitar for my brother and a piano keyboard for my oldest sister. They were the most expensive items that had been asked for from the two that had been in the accident, which I felt was something they deserved.

A popular gift for girls in our age group were twirling batons. I wanted one so bad, and even my tomboy sister, Donna asked for one. We could see them under the tree with name tags identifying which one belonged to her and the other one for me.

Whenever mom and dad were out spending money like it grew on trees, we would dig the batons out from under the Christmas tree and play with them. Donna and I would dance around the living room, twirling our batons, like we knew what we were doing. We would accidentally hit ourselves in the head trying to impress one another with skills neither one of us had. By the time Christmas morning came, the only place the wrapping paper was left on those batons were the rubber end sections.

That year my aunt had given mom a pure white puppy, which she named Snowball. It was Christmas, and the ball of white fur reminded her of a snowball when it was curled sleeping, so the name seemed very fitting. We all loved that pup, but if anyone tried to claim him as their dog, mom quickly reminded us that he belonged to her. Our toddler at the time would often grab the tail and giggle as he dragged the puppy behind him. However, he would get a spanking for treating the dog badly.

This was the only time I felt as if we might have a chance in life with the massive number of gifts that were there. We had also restocked the shelves with food which was bought before the beginning of the month. The biggest turkey I had ever seen was put in the new freezer. It would be cooked for the big holiday meal at our grandparents'—a Christmas of cheer that would never be duplicated.

Soon the season changed. The lakeside community at my grandparents' offered a great deal of entertainment for all age levels of the grandkids. It is where I learned to swim and hung out with cousins who had made friends with the local kids.

Our oldest cousin, who lived with our grandparents, hung out with a few teenagers who played guitars, drums, and other instruments in their parents' garages. My brother had somewhat mastered some of the guitar skills with his new guitar —a skill we thought would forever be buried in his mind. He felt comfortable hanging out with them and proudly demonstrated his talents.

The local beach store had a covered patio and a concrete floor that had a walk-up window to buy candy, ice cream, and fountain drinks. I never had money to buy sweets and would offer to pick up trash for the owners in exchange for a few pieces of candy or an ice cream bar. I didn't need to steal to get candy and treats to share with my siblings. There was a lot of trash lying on the ground, and I worked to pick it up anytime we were there. I was the kid who had grape gumballs without the guilt now!

On Saturday nights, local bands would play some of the most popular rock and roll songs while teens danced and sang along. I was content to play with some of the cousins at the water's edge with the younger kids as we listened to the music. It was so much fun, and I enjoyed the rare moments in time when I could put my fears aside.

We didn't own a washer or a dryer, so trips to grandma's house were common to do our laundry. I would help my mom gather the multitudes of dirty clothes, bedsheets, and towels that piled up in the corners of all the rooms of the house, which ended up being more than our baskets could hold.

There would be so many clothes and too many kids to ever make the trip all at once. So, the loads would be transported in stages.

Baskets of laundry and some of the kids would make the first trip along with huge boxes of detergents to get mom started on the process, while the rest of the laundry would be transported in the next trip.

My grandparents set their wringer-type washer and the twin

tubs in the front yard for us to do the wash. Yep, we did laundry in the front yard with kids running around all over the place. There would be baskets of clothes scattered from the car to the washer. An extension cord was stretched from an outlet on my grandpa's back porch, along with a water hose to fill the washer and twin tubs. The hose would be used to change the water in between cycles. I think back now and wonder what the residents of this quiet community must have thought about all of us.

Mom would wash a few loads of clothes, most often in the same water, then she would open a valve to drain the water out of the washer. The water inside the washer would get so muddy. It was more like the consistency of chocolate milk as it came out. With each load, my mom would stuff that little washer just as full as she could get it. I have no idea how it was even possible for the agitator to move.

As the water drained out onto the ground, she would run clothes through the wringer's rollers in clumps. This would be more than it could handle, so the washer's safety lever would trigger it to shut it off so as not to destroy the rollers. She ran clothes from one twin tub to the other to rinse them. She swung the machine's wringer section over a basket after they were rinsed that would be taken home and hung on clotheslines to dry. By the time we finished washing all the clothes, grandpa would be very tired of having all of us there. Although my grandmother never said anything, I am sure she was glad to see the last of the baskets and kids loaded up and taken home.

One laundry day, we had taken all the clothes and kids to grandma's house, and mom had begun to sort out the whites from the colors, towels from the sheets, and so on. I started to sort out the clothes with her, so I could secretly inspect the small pairs of panties my sisters had worn. I wanted to see if there was any blood in them. It was my way to watch for signs in the event that my dad was doing anything to my little sisters. I had developed different ways to keep an eye out on the little girls, and this was something I did on a regular basis.

After she told me to get the laundry soap out of the car for her to start the first of many loads, I went to the car and looked for the soap in the back seat, then the front, and finally the back section of the station wagon. It was nowhere to be found. Standing at the back of the car, I yelled out to her, saying the soap was not in the car. She began to curse me as if it were my fault for leaving it at home.

Mom told me to let my dad know we had forgotten all the laundry soaps in the kitchen at home, and he would have to make the trip to get it. I did not want to tell him, so I directed Donna to go and tell him. She refused and went on about doing what she was doing. The fear of my having to go with him to pick up the soap began to sink in. I went inside and told him, and as predicted, I would have to go with him. He claimed he needed someone to run into the house, grab it and get back in the car so my mom could get the wash cycles started.

I sat in the back seat as we started the short journey to get the soap. He tapped his hand down on the front seat, telling me to climb over and sit up there with him. I told him that I didn't want to and just wanted to stay in the back and play with the kid's toys that were lying on the floor. He seemed to accept me staying in the back seat.

As we approached our driveway, our now fully grown dog Snowball had a visitor. We would chain Snowball to his doghouse when we were gone for the day, and a female dog from the neighboring farmhouse had come to visit him. Dad yelled at the dogs and honked the horn to interrupt the activity they were engaged in. I could not see what was going on, but I saw the visiting female dog run across the field.

I jumped out of the back seat and ran inside to find the boxes of laundry detergents. I found an opened box that was half full along with the new box mom had instructed me to bring back. I tucked the unopened box of soap under my arm and held the open box upright to not spill it as I began to exit the kitchen. Suddenly, I heard our dog yelp as if he were being hurt. I came running out the door to see what was going on with our pet. I discovered my dad was dragging him by his collar towards the house.

My immediate thought was dad was going to leave the dog inside the house while we were gone. I asked him what he was doing to Snowball, and dad replied by telling me about how puppies were made. Dad grabbed my arm as I tried to make my way past him, causing me to drop the opened box of soap as I watched it spill out all over the place.

He held my arm as he rolled our family pet on his back and began to explain the anatomy of our dog. Then, he began to demonstrate an activity that caused the dog to jerk around. I told dad to stop hurting him. Dad said the dog liked it, and he wanted me to watch as he fondled our family pet.

I was astonished he would go to that length with his twisted ways. I knew time was running out, and we needed to get back to my grandparents' with the soap. He drove us back, explaining I was the only one of his kids he would ever show that to. I wondered if he did this sort of thing all the time with our dog and wondered what he did to the girl dogs.

We made it back with the soap. I went inside to visit with my grandma, who was playing Yahtzee with some of the other adults. I sat in the corner and ate crackers with butter on them as they rolled the dice. After mom finished the laundry, which took most of the day, we made several trips back home.

Once we unloaded the kids, the clothes, and the leftover soaps, I was told to change my smaller brother's diaper. He was always mischievous and posed a challenge every time I would change him or give him a bath. I unpinned the big yellow duck diaper pins that were holding up his diaper. The pins were so big, and it was difficult for me to open. They were the only size that would go through the thickness of a double fold cloth diaper.

Can you imagine the shock I felt when I discovered a worm was coming out of his rectum when I took off his diaper? It extended four to six inches from his body. I called for my mom to look at it as he ran away from me and took off strutting through the house naked with this worm dangling from his butt!

I asked my mom, "Why was there a worm coming out of his butt?" It looked like a skinny nightcrawler that we would fish with at the lake. I ran to catch him so I could carry him butt first to show my mom. She didn't seem surprised by it at all. She told me to hold him still as she reached down and gently pulled it out of his rectum. I am guessing it was at least 10" long.

"I remember the house, the rooms, the worm, every little detail!"

If one of us had worms, we all had worms, according to my family's thinking. Oh my gosh, the brutal treatment methods my family would use. All of us would be treated for them but not under the care of a real doctor. The medicine of choice for that was a full tablespoon of plain white sugar with a few drops of turpentine on it. Yep, you read it correctly. TURPENTINE. Mom would pinch our noses as she forced our lips open to eat the mixture that would supposedly kill the worms that were crawling around inside of our intestines. Talk about disgusting. I would rather clean the pail of poopy diapers than eat this stuff!

It was what we did to rid our bodies of the slimy crawlers that were inside of us. Mom would look at the diapers to see if the dead worms were coming out when she changed the diapers in the days that followed the treatments.

Bad cases of head lice were common in the family where my mom would shift the blame to the school or our extended family for spreading them. The school's greasy shampoo handed out at times had such a strong odor that it stunk like a skunk. As bad as it smelled, it was far better than the family's "old wives tale" of treating it. Who would ever think it was a good idea to put "Diesel Fuel" in a person's hair as a preferred method to kill common transferable cases of headlice? It's what my family did because we were cut from a different cloth. Looking back, I am sure it was because we couldn't afford the drug store medicines.

It was such an endless cycle, that the school began to check our heads and then send us home when they discovered we had lice. We would not be allowed to return until they were gone.

I could handle the fact that we had bugs, except when my hair had grown down to my waist. My sister Donna and I would always compete with a few of our cousin's on whose hair was the longest. Our mom would cut off our hair to get rid of the bugs and the eggs they left behind. I would get so mad at her as I watched my hair float down to the floor with every cut she made. It seemed like every time my hair got long, she would cut it off because of the head lice.

When I look at some of my school pictures, I could tell if I had lice or not, depending upon my hair's length. Even though I hated it, I tried to find a good side. At least I didn't have to eat a spoonful of sugar and chemicals to get rid of worms!

chapter fourteen

Salt in Open Wounds

My mom's relationships with her siblings, my aunts were different from one to the other. She would trade True Story magazines she had read with one sister and talk about the different characters on the soap operas she watched. Mom would also carry gossip from one sister to another, which would often cause turmoil within the family. They would get upset with one another, and the visits would stop for a few weeks. They ultimately would resolve their differences, and the visits would resume. As kids, we enjoyed the visits, which gave us the opportunity to play with our cousins from different families.

One of my aunts and her husband frequently played Euchre and other card games with my mom and dad. She worked for a nursing home while my uncle worked at a local manufacturing factory in Kokomo, the city where they had lived for many years. My uncle had a heart attack and had to undergo surgery immediately. Afterward, he had to spend a few weeks off from work to heal. He soon felt well enough to go back to work. However, the company did not allow him to return to his job in the plant after having his heart attack, and they didn't offer him any options other than retirement. Reluctantly, and to maintain benefits for his family, he was forced to retire.

A heart attack will change your perspective on life. My uncle wanted to spend time with his eldest daughter and her family, who lived in Arkansas.

They decided that they would make the leap and move. They sold their house, packed up their belongings, and found themselves in the quiet little country town of Pangburn, Arkansas. They were content as they settled into their retirement life, but they missed family ties in Indiana. I had enjoyed being around my cousins, and when they moved it was heartbreaking for me.

It did not take long until my aunt called long distance to our house and planted the seed for us to relocate. They would be on the phone for what seemed to be hours catching up on the family gossip they were no longer a part of.

With the newfound wealth Mom and dad had, a big move like this could be a possibility. Dad was raised in the Ozark mountains' foothills, and a southern lifestyle would suit him fine. It would be hard for mom to move so far from her parents, but my aunt was very convincing. She made it sound like Arkansas was the promised land. A place without snow in the winter, and it would be cheaper to heat a home. They lived a different kind of life than we did and had luxuries we didn't have. Things like real heating and air conditioning!

Dad started making frequent trips to Arkansas. The goal was to find suitable housing for our family to live in, and I use the term "suitable" lightly. I could see the possibility of another move was in our future.

This would be the last move we would ever make as a family unit.

It would bring a lot of challenging times for all of us to endure. Paths I did not see coming, but would offer hope for the first time in my young life.

He came home from one of his trips with a big truck with wooden side walls and a makeshift gate to close the back of the bed. He must have gotten it in Arkansas because he had left a few days earlier in a car. The kids all gathered around and began asking questions about the truck with such excitement. It was an old red beat-up truck that would do well to transport our belongings to the house he had bought in Letona, Arkansas.

The plan was made to move in stages. For the first trip, we

would take some of the furnishings and some of the packed boxes from the house in Keawanna, along with tools, welding equipment and most of the stuff dad had collected over the years. All of us were excited about making a move to a different state. Dad had gotten funds from the lawsuit, so our living near our grandparents and the lakeside community was going to be left behind forever.

In the days that followed, dad and other family members helped load the back of the truck with items to be taken to the new house in the new state. With the truck's back gate closed, dad told my mom that I would be going with him and that we would be leaving very early the following morning. Then, he had me grab a few clothes to put inside the truck.

The last thing I ever wanted to do was to go on a trip that involved a truck. This interstate highway was going to be a lot greater distance than Cincinnati. All of the old memories came rushing into my mind.

My oldest sister began complaining to my mom about why it was always me who was picked to go on trips with dad. If she only knew how much pain and suffering I had gone through to protect our sisters from his perverted ways. How I had sacrificed myself to protect my siblings from being sent to foster homes. Or how I had protected her life and the lives of all our family members from his vivid threats. She had no clue that I hated going anywhere with him. She didn't know what went on in the dark of night while she laid peacefully sleeping.

The following morning as we drove out of the driveway, I looked back at my brother waving goodbye and told him that I would be back soon. We had created such a bond since the accident that only he and I can relate to.

As we drove down the highways of Indiana, crossing into the state of Illinois, we pulled into a parking lot I was all too familiar with. A truck stop. I was not sure what to expect as we pulled up to the gas pumps. We went inside, and I asked where the bathroom was while dad ordered some food to go.

I felt relieved as we got back into the cab of the truck, making an exit out of the truck stop with our bag of food, a cup of coffee for my dad, and a cup of sweet tea for me. Dad said we needed to make up some time as we continued the journey. We began eating our food as he kept driving. He started to tell me about the area and what to expect. I asked how far my cousins lived from our new place, where the school was, and the size of the house.

He began to mention points of interest along the route as we crossed over the Mississippi River on a massive bridge! I looked out the window at some of the long barges as we drove across the large structure of steel. It was the first time I ever saw a tugboat. That little boat was pushing a row of barges as it passed under the bridge.

This was a much longer trip than I had ever been on. We crossed the state lines of Illinois and Missouri and were quickly approaching Arkansas. The trip was long, and the truck wasn't the best ride. I was just looking forward to getting there. I wanted to see the new place which we would call home and my cousins!

The hours went by as I watched the highway road signs looking for the state line. Then suddenly, there it was: "Welcome to Arkansas." I assumed that once we got to the state line, that would be the end of the trip. But much to my disappointment, we still had miles to go. We drove up to a gas station to fuel the truck and make a bathroom trip.

I entered the building, holding on to my crotch to avoid peeing while I asked to be pointed to the bathroom. The lady at the counter pointed towards the back of the store and said: "You're gonna need the key," in a southern twang I could hardly understand. The only word I could understand her saying was "key," and it got my attention. She handed me the key as I made my way to the ladies' room. As I relieved myself, my feet dangling off the edge of the toilet, many things were going through my mind. Exciting things I had pictured in my mind about the little town of Letona. About the town of Searcy where I would be going to school. I had expected dad to force me to do things to him as he typically did when he had me alone. But, I never imagined what he would do to me when we got to the house.

It was late in the evening when we drove into this tiny little town that had very few homes along the roadway. There was a dim light glowing from the only store on the main street as we drove past. It served as the local country store where a pack of cigarettes cost twenty-six cents and was also the post office for zip code 72085.

Dad pulled into the front yard aiming the headlights towards the house we were going to live in. I could not believe what I was looking at. This place looked as if it had been used as a tool shed, not a house. As I got out of the truck, I asked him where the bathroom was. He looked down at me and said, it was an outhouse and it is in the back of the lot and told me to just squat down in the yard somewhere.

Dad brought in an old camping lantern to light up the inside of the house. He sat it on the floor as he entered, giving me a better view when I came inside for the first time. I picked up the lantern and carried it as I toured the house from room to room, trying to define what each of them was.

There was an old metal cabinet with what appeared to be a sink in it, but it didn't even have a faucet in it. It was missing one of its doors, and a few items were stored there, which I could not identify. The cabinet was the only indicator that this was the room that would serve as the kitchen. Then I saw the chimney flue where the wood-burning stove would sit, and I could tell it would take up a lot of the space and guessed that would be the living room. The last room would be the only bedroom for all eleven kids to share. The spoiled brat, (my oldest sister) would freak out when she found out she would be sharing a room with everyone.

This is the suitable housing dad had bought with the

settlement money they had been given! A three-room shack that did not have plumbing. As I walked through the house carrying the lantern, I wondered if this place even had electricity. I looked up at the ceiling, saw a light fixture without a bulb, and noticed a switch on the wall beside the front door. I asked dad if we had a light bulb for it, and he told me the power had not been turned on yet. That explained why we were using the lantern!

What the heck? How could a family of thirteen possibly live here?

The floors had so much dust on them, it was hard to tell what they were made of. I could tell that they were not fit to let kids crawl on. At least the house in Kewanna had all the necessities for a family and had linoleum floors. I didn't think mom was going to like this house.

At least the house in Westfield, with its bare walls and snow coming into the cracks during the winter, was better than this one. The place they had to condemn in Macy was small, but it had a toilet and running water. My best guess is this one could not have been more than four hundred square feet. There were no cabinets to store the multitude of dishes we had, not to mention the pots and pans. I wondered where the groceries would be stored on food stamp day as dad began to unload some of the items from the back of the truck.

This was the place dad had made several trips down from Indiana over the past few weeks that he had bragged about paying cash for. The dump he had been fixing up before we moved down permanently. He said he was going to build a bathroom and put in a toilet and a kitchen sink but would first have to dig a hole for a septic tank. I liked the house back home better, and I didn't want to move to this place.

I watched dad go outside the front door holding up his hand over his eyes, blocking the beam of the headlights as he walked towards the back of the truck. He carried in a metal bed frame and three pieces of wood, which he took into the bedroom. He placed the slats across the bed frame and wrestled a set of coiled springs, which he dropped onto the frame. Then he began to drag a mattress off the back of the truck to the front porch and told me to push on the other end to get it inside the door and onto the bed.

He turned off the truck's headlights as we began to settle in. He showed me an artesian well located on the back porch. It had a galvanized stove pipe modified to pull water out of the hole in the ground. A few feet of rope tied to a makeshift handle of the pipe had been nailed to the wall to prevent it from falling into the well and lost forever. I couldn't stand the smell of the water that was coming from this hole, and didn't want to believe that this was the water we would have to drink.

After the long day of traveling and the excitement in seeing the house wore off, I was exhausted. Sleeping arrangements came into mind, and the picture was becoming clear to me as I began fearing the worst. Dad carried in a small table and placed it beside the bed to put his cigarettes and lighter on. He had an old pie pan he had found to use as an ashtray.

The only items we had for the night was dad's leftover coffee he had from the truck stop, the tea I had not finished, and a few food items such as canned meat and a loaf of bread that mom had sent with us.

Carrying the lantern, I went out to grab the clothes I had thrown in the seat. Dad found a dirty smelling bedspread in some of the stuff he unpacked and threw on the mattress. When I came back into the room, I noticed a box of salt sitting on the table, and I thought it was odd. My leftover cup of tea was sitting beside it, so I discounted it as being nothing.

Then he told me I would be sleeping with him! My heart sank, and utter fear came over me as I began to tremble. He told me to take off my clothes, but I left my underwear and undershirt on like I would do when going to bed at home. "What is he going to do to me this time?" I thought as he picked me up and laid me on the bed. He turned off the lantern as I watched him unbuckle his belt. The room became so dark I could not see what he was doing, but I could hear his pants fall to the floor. I saw him take a final puff from the cigarette he was smoking as he reached over for the box of salt. He pulled away from the bedspread and reached in, grabbed my panties, and removed them. I begged him to please quit touching me that way and that I did not like it. But, it didn't matter how much I pleaded; he had a plan.

He had poured salt into his hand and he rubbed it all over my vagina. As it began to burn, I asked, "Why are you doing this to me?" Without getting an answer, he moistened the salt with some of the tea I had been sipping on all day. The salt began to burn tremendously as I started to make sounds from the burning pain. He told me not to yell as the salt would distract me with what he was about to do. He held his hand over my mouth, and violently raped me for the first time when I was only 12 years old.

"I remember the house, the room, what I was wearing, every little detail."

With all the pain I was feeling, I did not cry. I simply wanted to die. I kept saying to myself, "I wish I had never been born". Afterward, he went through his usual cycle of threats and gave me the bedspread to curl up with. I quietly laid there, thinking about how afraid I was of him. The simple act of crying made me fear that he would do something to hurt me. But at this point, what could be worse?

The burning from the salt and the pain he inflicted on me lasted throughout the night as I laid there, listening to my dad snore and sleep peacefully as if nothing had happened. I had trouble sleeping, and I knew this was going to be the beginning of a new line of events I would have to live through. What was left of my childhood was destroyed. I would continue to be the sacrificial lamb if this meant he would never destroy the innocence of my younger sisters' childhood with the terrible acts that he had forced on me for the last six years. I would do this if it protected them from all of the pain and mental stress he put me through at such an early age. It was an endless night of "what ifs" for me to think about.

I could never have imagined that this trip would be the end of the most innocent treasure a girl is given—her virginity. I never made the connection that he had stolen that precious thing from me long ago when I discovered blood in my underwear. Something God had given me was taken from me, and there was never a sense of remorse. This must have been what dad was preparing me for by fondling with his little finger and transitioning to his thumb. Intercourse was the next step in his plan. I knew then: I had to keep my sisters away from him at all costs.

The following day my aunt and her family came over to help my dad unload the rest of the furniture we had brought down. I was so glad to see my cousins and hug them for the first time in what seemed like years. Stuff was stacked everywhere, and there was still a lot more to move down from Indiana.

How would all of us fit into this tiny house was beyond what I could comprehend. After the truck was unloaded, dad and I left to go back to Indiana. I would have to conceal the pain within my heart as we drove the long and quiet trip home.

There were no questions to ask and no words to be spoken

as we drove past the points of interest, crossed state lines and bridges, as we headed north. My mind could not focus on the sites that were so fascinating to me before, but there would be other memories to be made in this lazy little town of Letona.

chapter fifteen

Lazy Letona

After a long goodbye from the family, it was time for the big move to Arkansas! With the truck loaded with the rest of our belongings and a beat-up station wagon packed with kids, we headed South!

My brother wanted to ride in the truck with our dad. Having enough space for two of the kids, he let both of us ride with him. Having my brother in the cab of the truck with us made me feel safe during this trip.

After one quick stop during our six hundred mile trip to the house, we found our way to the shack. This was the first time my mom saw the house, or lack thereof. She was mad at my dad and it started an argument that lasted for days. She hated the fact that it did not have indoor plumbing.

This lazy, laid-back little town did not live up to her expectations. Mom was looking forward to living near a town, unlike our previous houses. But, dad hadn't told her there was no town, the house did not have plumbing nor the condition of the structure. I knew mom would not be happy here.

Mom had no idea how small the house would be, so she brought everything but the kitchen sink with us on this move. We began unpacking some of the family belongings, storing many of the boxes in a shed at the back of the grounds. A place we called home consisted of Lots 11 and 12, in the Town of Letona, as described on the property deed and sold to my dad in the amount of $1,500.00 cash.

Mom questioned my dad about all the money they had gotten from the settlement. She began accusing dad of wasting it by playing poker with his buddies before the move. There was so much money that could not be accounted for. All she knew is we had a beat-up old truck, a station wagon that was running on fumes of gas (and no gas station in town), and tires so worn out that there weren't any treads on them. It was ready for the junkyard, and we were broke.

We unpacked the broom and the mop bucket as we all began to clean the floors. They were plywood and had areas that would splinter. I used the metal pancake turner to scrape off the mud while mom mopped. There was not a lot you could do to floors like that. That was when I started wearing socks all the time and made the little ones wear them, too.

We wiped off the sink as my dad and uncle carried in the stove and refrigerator. The electricity had been turned on and dad had requested a phone be hooked up to satisfy my mom's desire to gossip. They plugged in the refrigerator and hooked up the gas stove. They carried in the kitchen table and chairs and a wardrobe to be used as a pantry.

As I stacked stuff into the bedroom, I was reminded of events that had taken place here. The box of salt was still sitting on the table beside the bed. A bed that I refused to sleep on. I would have rather slept in the shed by the outhouse than to spend another night in that bed.

The living room began to take shape as we set up our mom and dad's bed in the corner, and we put the small TV under the windowpane. Although we still had kids in diapers, there was no need for a baby bed anymore. They would sleep in between the older kids on the beds while some of us found spots on the wooden floor.

Our aunt, who had convinced my mom and dad to move down here after they had retired, lived a few miles away. The offers of the promised land in the hills of Arkansas had begun to take shape as my uncle put his foot down right from the beginning that we would not be allowed to do our laundry at their house. We had no washer so a galvanized tub and a toilet plunger would be the method used to wash clothes here—a job I would have to do. Imagine that!

There was another wooded area in the back of the property, which my brother claimed as being his. Once we were settled in, he began to create an area that brought back memories of "the fort." He dug through dad's tools and junk and found nails, a hammer, and even some rope to recreate his childhood memory. He worked long and hard to reconstruct what was long gone. Stick and stones would reshape the area, making it a place for his buried treasures and a place we would all enjoy, including our cousins who helped build it.

Mom found friendship with a family who lived blocks away just off the main road. They had two sons that my brother befriended soon after we moved into the area. Their mom, Edwina or Eddie for short, became a friend of the family except for our dad. She did not like him at all. She had good instincts!

Eddie had suffered from polio and had a few deformities, but they did not slow this woman down. She cleaned and cooked for her family like a normal housewife would. Her house was immaculately clean, and had a few bedrooms and indoor plumbing.

We added thirteen new residents to this tiny community that had a population of 201 displayed on the town sign. I remember saying, "We just added 13 more people!" everytime we passed it. It was where everyone knew everyone and their business. They all knew the condition of the old house and could not believe this big family had moved in. The previous owners had lived there for a long time and didn't have the money to invest in improvements. They must have been as poor as we were.

Eddie loved playing cards and board games. Soon, she began to host card nights with mom and allowed the older kids to play. My oldest sister scouted out the boys in town, and Eddie's house seemed to be the neighborhood favorite place to find them. She was the cool mom who let the older kids hang out, some of whom were her nephews.

A few months after we moved in, she wanted to tour "the shack" as she called it. So, I guess I got it right when I labeled it "the shack" the first time I saw it. She told my mom when she walked in that my mom should have shot my dad for bringing his family into this house. She looked into the rooms and asked where did all the kids sleep? Mom simply replied, "Wherever they want, except for the bed in the living room."

School was going to start soon, so my aunt drove our mom into town where she enrolled us in the school in Searcy. The only bus stop would be at the town's post office. Whenever I attended a new school, I tried to enjoy the few days before they figured out that we were the poorest family in school. During that time, we weren't called names and treated differently by the teachers and staff—it was kind of nice when even the kids did not know how destitute we were.

I hadn't been able to make any friends in all the elementary schools I had attended. Kids were quick to discover that we were part of a group that got free lunches. We had a few distant cousins in the same school who didn't want others to know that they were related to us because they were embarrassed. I understood. We were poor and they weren't. Heck, even I was ashamed of the way some of my family members acted.

I had to learn how to understand what people were saying with their southern accents. It reminded me of the lady at the gas station who said "yr" instead of 'you are.' It was the same old story in a different school, but it would become a place of resources to me in a few short years.

Dad did what he had always done: mechanical and welding jobs for people in the area, especially in Letona because no one else could weld and do odd jobs.

Our family was given a couple of horses from a deal my dad made doing work for a resident in the area. We named the taller of them Peanut, a chestnut-colored horse with a white patch on his face. We called the shorter one Smokie, a solid black horse that I could reach the top of his head to pet. He was short and wide, where Peanut was tall and slimmer.

We didn't have a saddle to put on either of them. All we had was a bridle that was messy to insert into his mouth, but it was the steering wheel. I was so determined to ride Peanut and I was going to try anything I could to be able to get on this darn horse by myself.

I scanned the area around the house and in the yard, and spotted an old wooden chair. With the bridle in his mouth, I led Peanut behind me and walked towards the chair. I aligned the horse with the back of the chair against his side while holding on to the bridle straps. I carefully stepped on the chair to mount the horse. Trying to balance myself on this rickety old frame and grabbing a hand full of his mane, I could barely make a mild leap to get my leg up and over the back of the horse.

I did it! I was on this horse, and I was able to get on it by myself. I held onto the leather straps, made the necessary sounds with my mouth, and nudged the horse with my heels into his side. That's all it took for this stupid horse to rev up and start to buck. I was thrown up in the air and landed on the very chair I used to get on the darn thing.

It hurt so bad when I landed on the chair— the legs broke and crumpled onto the ground with me. Peanut took off down the road with the bridle straps dangling from his mouth. I yelled out to my oldest sister, telling her that her horse had gotten loose and was out of the yard.

She came running out of the house. She was confused as to how the horse had gotten out of the yard with a bridle in his mouth. "I dunno," I explained as she ran down the road to retrieve him. As she captured the animal, I confessed that it was my fault that he had gotten away and that my attempts to ride him had failed miserably. I was in so much pain from being thrown off, I was barely able to walk.

Unknown to me at that time, some of the family members were watching me all along. They had watched the entire sequence with the balancing act with the chair as well as Peanut bucking me off. They were laughing at me so hard as I limped into the front door. It took me nearly an hour to get on that stupid horse for a ten-second ride.

After that, I stuck to riding Smokie. A horse who was short and easy to mount from the concrete front porch. The old wooden chair ended up in the woodpile and was later burned in the fort fire pit.

It was a moment where I had suffered physical pain. Still, more importantly, I had achieved something, and I felt a sense of satisfaction. I had gotten on that horse for the "first and last time" that day.

As time went on, I became tired of the endless abuses and stress that went along with keeping my family safe. I began to wonder why I was the only one who seemed to care. Then, I would look around the room at my sweet little sisters and remember what I was protecting. I looked at my little brothers and watched them play in the dirt knowing I would soon have to give them a bath in the galvanized tub that sat underneath the tree in the backyard.

The giggles they made when I would use a bowl to dump water over the tops of their heads as I watched the dirt run from their bodies along with the smelly well water brought joy to my heart.

I would stare at this petite woman I called mom and wondered what made her the person she was or what had gotten her to the point of hating some of her kids. What had they done to deserve that kind of treatment? They were just kids. I kept them away from her, but you could still see the hate she had towards them. I was thankful that I could protect all of them from one form of abuse or another.

I watched as my dad worked at trying to get running water inside the house. He spent hours digging a huge hole in the backyard where a septic tank would go. I wondered why he did all the things he had done to me. Why was I his favorite, and why was I called the prettiest little girl he had? I did not feel special in any way. My oldest sister was the prettiest girl in the family.

But God had a path for me, and I didn't even know it. The path was going to become very clear in a few short months! A path that would lead me to a power that I didn't know existed. The same power that was giving me strength all these years to protect the kids. Soon I realized that the evil deeds were not in the walls of the houses we lived in, but in the hearts of the adults that lived with us. Their evil never needed to be packed in a box to move it; it was rooted inside their hearts!

chapter sixteen

The Labor of Redemption

Dad had acquired a plot of ground just over eight acres located a few miles from the house for only $10.00. The land was beside a railroad track and had never been used for anything. He planned to plant the field with potatoes, which was a primary source of food for us. French fried or mashed, and potato pancakes were some of the ways we prepared them. Still, fried potatoes with onions were the favorite even among the little kids.

We were the farmhands and spent hours upon hours picking up the bigger rocks and stacking them along the tracks. Then, we used big spoons to plant the field. Row upon row, the kids would dig a hole and drop in a small slice of seed potato and then used a ladle of water to moisten the dry, dusty mounds we had created.

The heat of the Arkansas sun was so hard to bear that by the time we came home, we were hot and exhausted. No time for a bath in the shade, I had to help cook.

When I came inside, I would sit on a kitchen chair and start peeling potatoes for dinner. I remember my dad walking by me as I was using a small paring knife to peel them. He smacked me on the side of the head and told me to quit peeling them so thick because I was wasting them. I did not care how I peeled them. After they were all peeled, I sliced them into small sections for the frying pan. I had spent hours planting eight acres of the darn things, and my hands were chapped from slicing the seed potatoes out in the hot sun!

One of dad's ways of making money was to buy and sell fruits and vegetables from the back of the truck. He would take a few of the kids to go pick watermelon, cantaloupe, and bushel baskets of tomatoes, and sell them along the side of the road and at the local mom and pop stores. After all, money was money and with this many kids to help, it kept the lights on.

Sleeping in the one-bedroom at night, I would hear my oldest sister and brother sneaking out of the window located beside a metal closet our friend had given us. This was out of view of mom and dad's bed in the living room. They would raise the window slowly as it squeaked while whispering among themselves. I would raise my head as I watched them crawl out the window and use a stick to keep it up so when they came back, they could crawl in. My sister would threaten to beat me up if I told on them. My brother always defended me—he knew that I would not tell on them. My sister bullied me all the time, and she believed that I would be tempted to rat her out if asked about it.

They were sneaking out to meet up with friends and go to a place called, The Bluff Hole. It was a beautiful natural spring with a pond area surrounded by steep rocky bluffs. Trees surrounded the area, and one of them had a branch with a rope attached for swinging out over the watering hole. There was a clear area where teens would park their cars, listen to radio music, and have campfires near the water. It was a place to hang out and drink beer.

It was the entertainment hub of this little town, and we would often ride our horses down to it and play on the rope swing plunging into the cool waters. I was a scaredy-cat and never attempted to swing on it. I was fine with just walking into the water on my own. Sometimes one of the older neighborhood kids would pick me up and throw me in.

There was a trail that led up to the edge of the cliff. I never made it to the top because of the poison ivy and oak that grew all year round. We had a lot of fun at the watering hole, and if we were not at home, most likely we were there.

As time went by, my oldest sister became pregnant by one of the local boys. Apparently, drinking beer and swinging off the rope was not all she was doing when sneaking out at night. Her being pregnant gave her every reason to be lazier than ever. Suddenly,

I was making her peanut butter sandwiches and lighting her cigarettes on the stove. Now there was a need to set up a baby bed in the living room again. Most of my siblings were now "outhouse" trained, and I had no intentions of changing diapers again.

It was the repetition of the many years when we had lived in Indiana and mom was at a hospital having babies. When my sister went into labor, mom stayed with my sister in Heber Springs while she was giving birth, which gave my dad the opportunity to rape me in the bed that he and mom shared. There were kids sleeping on the floor while others slept in the bedroom.

Soon after my sister had her son, our entire family made a trip to Indiana to see the grandparents. We were planning to spend a few weeks there during the summer and dad brought a load of fruits and vegetables to sell while we were there. My sister, a new mom, commented that she would not be returning when we had arrived, and she did not. She met a guy a few years older than her and soon we were planning a wedding all within a few weeks. We would be returning to Arkansas with two fewer passengers than we had come with. She had always mistreated me, and I was fine with leaving her behind.

It was great to return to the lakeside community where my grandparents still lived. Many kids had grown up and moved out of the area. An uncle had started a trash route there, and everyone knew him. I began to hang out with an older crowd. The bridge that spanned across a narrow section of the lake didn't seem to be so high after all and I became braver and braver as I watched kids jump off it. Eventually, I finally jumped off the bridge and into the water with other kids.

It was a great summer that went by fast, and I hated the moment we had to say our goodbyes all over again. I sat in the car's front seat with my mom while a couple of my brothers rode with dad in the truck. I was the kid who had to sit in the back, so sitting in the front seat was rare for me. We stopped at a grocery store and bought a pound of bologna and a loaf of bread to eat as we made our way home.

At this time, I was 14 and my life of abuse would continue as I grew older. During my childhood years, I endured some of the most horrific sexual abuse. I was forced to do adult level sexual acts, some of which were so demented that I will not share them. This was my living hell, and it had gone on for nearly a decade!

It seemed as if there was no hope for me. I felt lost and alone without a sense of purpose. Yeah, I found pride in the job I was doing in cleaning the house, cooking, and helping with kids. My brother and I became even closer once our sister stayed in Indiana, and he was all I had.

But what did I do to deserve this kind of life to have a mom and dad like they were? I wasn't able to figure out how to escape this horrible life. I knew I could not abandon the family because I felt that I was protecting children and keeping mom from beating them. I was also too scared to confide in anyone. I felt as if my only option was to wait until I was old enough to move out.

I suffered abuse because so much fear had been instilled in me by my dad and his threats. He had convinced me that he would hurt my family and me if I ever told anyone, and I believed him. He beat on my mom and whipped the other siblings, and I took him at his word when he said he would KILL them!

I felt that I was the one who had to protect them. All of them! Especially my younger sisters, I could not let him do this to them and destroy their lives. It was how my mind operated. There were four of them that I wanted to protect at all costs.

"I did not want any of them to live the life that I was already living!"

This had become the burden and the cross that I carried for my family. At that time, I didn't know about the burdens of Jesus Christ and how vital faith would become in my life.

Until one day, all of that changed!

It was a hot summer day and mom was at our friend Eddie's house playing cards. I was washing clothes in the tub in the backyard. I was using the plunger to agitate the clothes to wash them and pull clean water from the well to rinse them as best as possible. Donna and I would hold the clothes between us as she twisted one end of them in one direction. I twisted in the opposite direction to wring out most of the water before hanging them on the clotheslines. Blue jeans were particularly hard to do. We laughed at one another as we challenged each other to see who could squeeze out the water faster.

Donna had gone inside the house as I began to plunge a full load of jeans. I would walk around the round tub pressing down on the clothes to get them wet using very little soap, which was hard to rinse off. I would make a few trips around the tub, plunging the clothes until my arms started to ache. I yelled for Donna to come out and help me wring them out, but she didn't respond. I wanted to get this done, and my patience wore thin waiting for her to come and help.

I thought she might have gone to get a bucket of water from the well, so I peeked my head inside the door, and she was not there. I walked to the front yard to see if she might be out there. All I saw were some of the smaller kids playing in the ditch along the road.

Then I walked inside the front door and discovered my dad forcing himself onto my sister, who was just one year younger than me. I thought I had been protecting her from this!

My heart sank! I was so mad and devastated for her.

I yelled at him to let her go and told her to "come with me" as he got up from the chair and chased me out the door, keeping her in his grip.

"I remember the house, the room, what she was wearing, every little detail!"

I did not know what to do! He yelled at me as I ran off the front porch, filled with a huge range of emotions that were going through my mind! She was the sibling who was the most defiant member of the family and the one my mom physically abused. It never occurred to me that he was sexually abusing her! I felt I had failed to protect her from him!

It began to make sense to me why she seemed mad at the world all the time. My dad was telling her the same things all along. She hadn't said a thing to me, and I never said anything to her. Like me, she was brainwashed with fear. "Don't tell, or I will hurt the family." "You're my favorite!" Neither one of us knew we were both living the same life of hell!

Later that evening, she and I started to talk about what had taken place. I began to ask her questions about how long he had been abusing her. I wanted to hear every little detail, but she didn't really want to talk about it. I watched tears form in her eyes and roll down her cheeks. I held her as she began to tell me how embarrassed she was at what I had seen that day. As she continued to cry, she asked me why mom hated her so much.

I didn't have any answers for her. I didn't tell her that I had been living the same kind of sexual abuse. This was her moment for her to share her emotions with me, and I let her.

That is when I realized my sacrifice had not stopped him from hurting her. I knew I had to do something soon before he began to cycle through the three younger daughters! The 4, 5, and 6-year-old. I was going to protect them at all costs. I had to come up with a plan to get him out of this house!

This is all that I thought about for what seemed to be a lifetime. This was my focus now. I had to draw on strengths I never knew I had, and this began the path of redemption for me.

chapter seventeen

Piece of My Heart

Donna was involved in gymnastics at school. I think she found her niche for gymnastics because of all the tumbling she had to do to get away from our mom at home. It was something that she was good at. The school had her on the gymnastics team, but we didn't have the money to support the demands of playing any sport at school. When the bell rang at the end of the day, after-school activities were not an option for kids who relied solely on buses for transportation to get home. It gave Donna an outlet from the events that she didn't know we had in common.

After I had discovered that she was sexually assaulted, she and I became closer. I began to watch her practice doing cartwheels, handstands, and a technique called a fish flop. I admitted to her that I didn't have that kind of talent, and I wished that she could travel with the gymnastic team to compete with the other girls.

At this school, a girl took the time to talk to me as a friend. Her name was Vanessa Atkins. She would bring me clothes that usually didn't fit because I was a runt. She would share the great lunches she brought from home, give me money for candy at the store across the street, and would allow me to copy from her homework assignments. Yes, I cheated on homework because I never had time for it, and if I did, it always resulted in bad grades.

We became the best of friends and talked about trips we would take when we got out of school. We said if we ever moved away from one another, we would meet up wherever our finger landed on the globe that we had spun around. She asked at what age we should plan to meet, and we both picked thirty.

Mom and dad never allowed me to spend the night away with anyone outside of our family. Vanessa would invite me time and time again to spend the night at her house where she lived, which was just outside of town. I had begged mom for weeks to allow me to ride the bus from school to Vanessa's house and stay overnight with her. Finally, my mom let me go, which would be a defining moment in my redemption path.

When I got there, I thought I had stepped into a rich person's house. There was a color TV, a bathroom with a tub, and dinner cooking on the stove. As we sat down at the table to eat, they reached out to hold hands to pray. I had never done this before and wasn't sure how to pray, but I listened to the words and it moved me in ways I had never felt before.

"I remember the house, the rooms, the food, every little detail!"

Her bedroom was just gorgeous, with soft tones of pink on the walls and ruffled curtains covering the window. I loved being there and could not imagine ever living in a place this nice. After we did some homework and took baths, we sat crossed-legged on her bed. We started talking about the kids in school, which included complaining about our teachers, who all had it out for us and, of course, the boy crushes.

She began asking me questions about my home life. She knew I was poor but did not know about the deepest secrets I had hidden from her. She knew nothing of my home life. There were things I just felt so ashamed of and did not want to share with anyone. She asked why I had not invited her to stay overnight at our house. I couldn't tell her about the living conditions at our house, and my fear of what my dad might do if I brought a girlfriend over to spend the night.

God puts people in your life for a reason. Vanessa was put into my life. I decided SHE was the one I could share my secrets with for the first time. I began to tell her about the sexual abuses I had been going through with my dad and how I most recently walked in and saw him abusing my sister. I told her I had been trying to get my mom to let me stay overnight with her for weeks so I could get out of there and that I had planned to get my dad out of the house.

She was shocked and started crying as I begged her not to say anything. I had to calm her down and convince her that I did have a plan! "Trust me. I have it all figured out." I kept pleading and forcing her to make a promise not to say anything to anyone. She wanted to wake her dad up and tell him immediately as she started to get off the bed and reach out for the door handle. It was all I could do to convince her to let me take care of it. As best friends do, she hugged me and agreed not to tell.

Well ... We all know how teenagers keep their promises, right?

I had made the critical choice to share my story with my friend, and now I was going to put the path of redemption in place. It gave me the strength I needed to talk to a teacher, the principal, anyone who would listen. I was ready to help protect my sisters, and I was going to do it now! THERE IS A PATH FOR ME. I had to follow it wherever it led, and I was determined to go down it.

The following morning Vanessa was so distraught she could not go to school, but I had to. The wheels were turning so fast in my mind as the bus slowly made its way to school. I went to our principal to talk about some of the things that were going on at home. I was petrified he would call my mom or dad to come to school. I didn't want to face them at all.

I bet I was not in his office for more than ten minutes, and I guess I had expected immediate action. I imagined that they would go get my dad right then! However, there was no real apparent response, and I felt so disappointed. I had no idea how things like this were handled! During some of the threats over the years, telling a teacher or anyone of authority would bring about negative results. But, I was ready to deal with it if it meant I could protect my family. Little did I know I would have to go back home that afternoon! This was not at all what I expected would happen!

A few days later, I was called to the office while at school. I was then taken to the local "Welfare Office." There I was assigned a "Caseworker." I wasn't sure what a caseworker was, but they introduced me to a woman named Keri. She was a very soft-spoken young woman with short hair and seemed perfectly put together. She told me that Vanessa had shared my secret with her family, and they called to make a report with their office.

This was going to be the moment when I was about to become the most hated member of my family. There was no turning back now. Life was going to change for all of us in a very dramatic way, and for the rest of our lives. I was ready to tell them everything. ALL OF IT! Even the way my mom was beating the kids!

Keri led me into a room that had a table and a few chairs in it. In her soft-spoken voice, she asked if I wanted something to drink as she laid her notepad down on the table. I said no, but she gave me a glass of water anyway. So, with a uniformed officer in the room, she began to ask questions and take notes.

I started from the beginning and told her about the abuse that started in Indiana. She asked how old I was at the time and explained that I thought I was six going on seven. I could remember the house we lived in, the school I was attending, and even told her what I was wearing. I began to tell her how scared I was to be there, and if dad found out, he would kill me. I told her all about the threats he made to harm my family. I told her how he said we would be taken away to foster homes and never to see one another again. I couldn't imagine life without my siblings.

I was afraid, but I wanted to tell her everything. I stressed how important it was to me that we weren't taken to a foster home. I just wanted her to get my dad out of the house. She began to explain that foster homes were places where kids were treated well and that there were many great things they could do for the rest of my family and me. I would defend my opinion on what I had been told about them being a bad place to live. I didn't want anything to do with the idea of going to a foster home. She calmed me down by saying," I will do everything I can to help you."

I spent many school days at the Welfare Office, spending most of the hours there when my mom and dad thought I was in the classroom. I was giving them every little detail then going back home like normal. You know, the everyday routine of kids, cooking, and cleaning. This went on for a while for them to build a case against my dad. I didn't know what "building a case" was, I just heard them say it a few times. Finally, after weeks of telling them all that I had been through, I told them that I had also seen him forcing himself on to my sister Donna.

One afternoon, they brought me to the Welfare Office to meet with Keri. She told me that they were going to have my dad arrested and that they were going to leave the kids with mom, "FOR NOW." I never imagined my mom would become my enemy, but she did, and so did the rest of the family.

I was so glad to hear that they were taking my dad away, and during the bus ride home I felt relieved that I would not have to spend another night with him there. It would be the only moment of gratification I would get from this entire sequence of events. Our dad was arrested, and of course, the whole town knew all about it.

My oldest brother met me and the rest of the school age kids at the bus stop and told us that dad had been taken to jail. I acted as if it was a surprise to me, and I questioned him about what mom was doing. He told me she and the rest of my siblings had been crying all day.

I began to question if I had done the right thing or not. I hadn't considered the emotional impact this would have on them. To me, I was protecting them. But they loved him, and so did my mom—even though he beat her all the time. They hadn't experienced the kind of abuse Donna and I had been through. As I picked up the youngest little girl and held her as she cried, I knew deep down that I had done the right thing even as her tears fell.

They were so hungry that I began to make a batch of Hobo bread to feed everyone. My brother began to flatten out the dough as the iron skillet started to heat. It was enough to get their attention as mom curled up into a ball on her bed.

It was on a Friday when they arrested my dad, and oddly enough, I was grateful. I needed to be there for my family. The following day mom would get out of bed long enough to smoke a cigarette and crawl back into bed. I kept the kids out of her way and cooked whatever we had to feed them. Neighbors started to bring in food to help us, but mom barely got out of bed to thank them.

In the days after they took my dad and had left the kids with my mom, they kept bringing me to the Children Services Office to give them updates about the situation at home. They asked me if my mom was cooking for us or cleaning the house. Of course, she wasn't, and the words "FOR NOW" started to sink in.

After the initial shock wore off, they began to send out caseworkers to check on the ten kids' wellbeing. Mom alone was responsible for all of us, and she had no source of income. She would clean the house for the scheduled visits and have the kids somewhat cleaned up when they got there.

Mom became very distraught very quickly the following weeks after dad had been arrested. She started to tell the kids that it was all my fault that their dad was in jail. The little ones didn't know why he had been taken away. They didn't even understand what jail was. She was so hateful to me, but I didn't care. I was going to keep her from beating my little brothers and sisters. I was determined not to let her near them anymore.

The phone was eventually turned off from lack of payment on the high phone bills with all the long-distance calls she had been making to Indiana. Without any means of communication to her family, who had been consoling her, she eventually broke. She loaded all the kids in the car, except me, of course, and was driving around town threatening to drive off a cliff. She was threatening to kill all of them.

I ran to the neighbors and told them what she was doing, and asked them to call my caseworker. I was not going to let her hurt my siblings. I had done too much over the years to protect them, and I was not going to let her harm them now. The police finally showed up, and she was eventually arrested for child endangerment, abuse, and neglect. The return visits I had been making to the Welfare Office provided them with enough information that they could build a case against her as well. They just needed that one thing to arrest her, and this was it.

I tried to comfort my crying little siblings. They rejected me, but I did what I could for them anyway. I felt so sorry for them, but not for my mom. She was so cruel, and at this point, I was relieved that they were taking her away. Without an adult in the house, my worst fears were coming true. We were going to Foster Homes.

"FOR NOW," was here!

There were no options left. My mom was not fit to take care of any of us! We had ten kids, ages 16 and under living in a one-bedroom house! They sent a different Case Worker other than mine to the house that afternoon. There were too many kids to find homes for all of us on such short notice. My younger sister Cathy had been spending a lot of time with a family who lived on the outskirts of town.

They took an interest in Cathy, and offered to house five of the kids for the night. Our aunt had the youngest at her house in Pangburn, which we all figured she would keep because she was her favorite niece. The rest of us were allowed to stay at our friend Eddie's house. The children's services would have to eventually find homes for all of us "except for the sibling that is 350 days older than me".

I had failed to protect my family from being separated, but I knew my little sisters would not have to live the life I already lived. It felt good knowing that, but I felt guilty at the same time.

"That is where I was mentally in all of this: at peace, but was I really?"

chapter eighteen

Dividing Times

The following day, two case workers came to gather the younger group of kids, and I met them at the house. Our aunt was instructed to bring my baby sister to Letona from her house in Pangburn. She was to be taken to a foster home along with the rest of us. With the younger tier of kids being divided from the older tier, it was time to see what path our lives would take. Being separated or divided, it all meant the same for me.

With all of us gathered at the house, our aunt, uncle, and even the cousins began to beg the caseworkers to let them keep our youngest sister, who was four at the time. They offered to be her guardian and do whatever it took to keep her. They refused! The case worker said that if the child stayed with my aunt, our mom might have access to her once released from jail. Their office had determined mom was unstable and felt it would put our sister at risk in the custody of an immediate family member.

While my aunt continued to argue her case, I started to sort out clothing for each of them to take along with them. I began to make a stack for each of them on the living room bed. I collected a pair of socks, underwear, shirts, pants, and dresses for each of them. I had always laid out outfits for the school-age kids, so it was something that I thought I should do for them. I didn't understand all that was going on, and I felt like I was supposed to help them pack some of their clothes to take with them.

There were cockroaches in the house, and one of the case workers told me politely that they were going to buy them all new clothes and I didn't need to pack them each a bag. It was her way of telling me they did not want the bug-ridden clothes in their cars.

My aunt and her family lost the argument for keeping my little sister. My uncle asked if they would be given enough time to leave the house, stating it would be too hard for their kids to witness them taking us away, which they agreed to do.

As my uncle began to back their car out of the driveway, my aunt started yelling and cursing at the Case Worker for not letting them keep their niece. If you knew my aunt, this was typical behavior for her when being challenged.

I held my baby sister, telling her to wave goodbye to them as they drove away. I could see our two cousins crying and waving goodbye from the back window. It would be the last time I would see them for many, many years.

From one heartbreaking moment to another, it was time for the upper tier of kids to say our goodbyes to the younger siblings. It was time for them to leave as they were loaded into the cars. They were crying, saying they wanted their mom. It was hard for me to understand and to watch because they viewed their mom from a different lens than I did. They didn't know any other life than the one they had been living. None of us did.

The only life they had experienced was being dirty little kids who played in the dirt and went to bed at night without being bathed. They had witnessed the many fights our mom and dad had when I was not at home to huddle them into a corner. But, this was normal for them. Everything I had done from a very early age to protect them over the years had come down to these last few moments.

Myself and four of my siblings stood in the middle of the road as we watched them drive away, passing the little store where I would walk with them. I think all of the people who lived along the road were watching from their windows as they drove by their houses with my family. The cars disappeared from our view as they drove around the curve, making their way out of town.

We looked at each other, knowing all of our lives had just changed forever. Our family unit of sibling life was over just like that. It would be our turn to say goodbye to each other in the days to come. I did not cry as we walked back into the house. We would stay with neighbors and Eddie until they were able to find foster homes for the rest of us.

I had been dealing with many personal female problems. One of the case workers had made arrangements for me to be seen by a doctor at the hospital in Searcy. They suspected I might have had infections from the sexual encounters I had been subjected to. Walking into the exam room, I had no idea what to expect. I had not been to a doctor or a hospital in many years. I felt afraid as I scanned the room that housed the medical equipment. It would be the first time I would have a female physical of this nature. After the exam and some testing, as expected, I had a severe infection. I didn't have a medical record, and no one knew if I was allergic to any medication. The attending doctor ordered an antibiotic, which would require a scratch test on my arm with a drug to make sure I was not allergic to it.

The nurse entered the room with a syringe with a huge needle attached to it. I am sure my eyes told them they were in for a fight. I was afraid of needles from early childhood illnesses and vaccinations, which I had to take. I fought like a wild cat as they held me down while telling them that they were not going to stick that thing in my arm. It took a few staff members to hold me down so they could scratch the surface of my arm with the needle expelling some of the medicine.

I felt like an idiot for fighting them for such a small scratch. It would not have left a scar had I calmly sat still, letting them do it. After a few minutes and no allergic reaction, they gave me a shot with so many drugs. It caused a huge bruise to form on my butt that hurt way worse than the scratch test. But I was embarrassed by my behavior, so I laid perfectly still, taking deep breaths as they injected the medicine.

I was taken back to Letona while I waited for word on our future foster homes. Eddie explained that older kids were harder to find homes for, but we were content to stay with her. Unfortunately, that wasn't an option no matter how much we pleaded with her. Soon, we would be met with the same kind of fate as the younger kids.

Later that week, a case worker came to take the kids that were below the age of 16. Cathy would stay at the home where she had been staying, and the oldest brother being sixteen, was allowed to stay with our friend. They were happy to accommodate at least one of us until the family would get there from Indiana. Three of us hugged our oldest brother and got into the back seat of the car as it was our turn to wave goodbye from the back window.

An older couple that owned a farmhouse and a barn full of horses would be our foster parents to keep the three of us together. They were a very kind and accommodating couple that had retired from the foster care program. But, they agreed to help out. Myself at fifteen, Donna at fourteen, and our brother, who was the thief among us at thirteen, became a real challenge for them in a very short amount of time.

From the first day we were there, we expected to help with the chores. We became farm hands again and worked alongside the couple to tend to the horses. None of us was very happy about getting up hours before school to work in the stalls and then clean up in time to get on the bus to go to yet another new school. It was nice to be together, but Donna would argue with the foster mother from the moment we got there. It was not the loving home life that the case workers had described to me. I had painted a different picture in my mind, but it was cleaner than where we had been raised; we had new clothes, and we were fed real home cooked meals.

Donna was told to go to her room for mouthing off after she was done with the dishes. Donna was trashing the bedroom and yelling out that she hated this place, and she was not going to do all the work. I went into the room and told her to stop yelling and tried to calm her down. I told her we were doing all the work at our house. At least there, we had a bed to sleep in and a tub to take a bath. She didn't care. She cried and said she did not like it here and wanted to go back home. It was then when I had to make her understand that we did not have a home anymore because of our dad.

Later that evening, she and I began to talk and shared stories about what our dad had done to us. She said he had started to mess with her when we lived in Keawanna. She explained once we moved to Arkansas, it got worse. She said he would wake her up in the middle of the night, forcing her to do some of the things that were all too familiar to me. Keawanna, I replied, telling her that I thought she was only nine when we moved there.

I began to share some of the nightmare experiences I had been through and how young I was when he first raped me. I gave her details about the time he had made me travel with him to bring down the first load of furniture to Arkansas.

She and I stayed up all night sitting on the bed talking about how we had both been living the same kind of hell. We were both too afraid to say anything to anyone because of the fears he had instilled into us.

"I remember the house, the room, the bed, every little detail."

I asked her if he told her that he would kill our mom and siblings, and she replied, "Yes." I asked why she would not listen to me when I would tell her to stop talking back when mom would be beating on her. Her reply stunned me! She said at least when mom would be hitting on her, she wasn't beating our younger brothers.

It was incredible to hear her say what I had been thinking for so many years about dad. I had justified it when he was sexually abusing me. At least he was not doing it to her or the rest of the girls.

It was a defining moment when two sisters who had existed in the same foster home had truly bonded for the first time. We had always played jump rope, hopscotch, and shared most household duties over the years, but we never really knew each other. The stories we shared that night about the sexual abuse were so similar, but the way our minds worked was the same without being aware of each other's truths. It was the most tender moment we ever shared and the first time in our young lives that we truly connected. A precious night between sisters I will always cherish.

The brother living there with us began stealing from the foster dad's wallet. How my brother ever thought that he would not be caught was beyond me. This couple did not have any other foster kids so it could have only been taken by one of us. The foster dad was so disturbed and upset that he called a case worker and requested that they take us out of the home.

We had been through so much over the past few days. Now we were going to have to go to yet another home. They sent us to school one morning with all of our clothes, where yet another case worker would pick us up at the end of the school day. As we walked out of the building together, we were all separated and taken away in three different cars as I wondered if I would ever see them again.

My sister Donna and I had formed a friendship, a real bond at this house and now it was going to being ripped right out from under us because of our brother's sticky finger. Once again, we could not be trusted. What else would be thrown at me as I tried to find some peace in these dividing times. However through it all, I would soon find out what peace really meant, because God had a path for me long before I ever knew it!

chapter nineteen

The Path is Clear

I was sent to a small town called Bald Knob. I had no idea
how the founders came up with that name, but it was where I
would be living for the first time in my life without a single sibling.
I was uncomfortable not knowing what that would be like, but I
had no control in deciding where I would live or with whom. I had
asked where they would be taking the other two, and I hoped in my
heart they would be together somewhere but knew deep down that
they would be a handful in any home in which they were placed. I
had asked where all the other kids would be living, but they would
not give me any details on their locations.

In Bald Knob I lived in a nice little white house located
in a neighborhood with sidewalks and a school that I would be

attending right down the block. The landscaping was beautiful, and it looked like a place I could only dream about living in. I compared this in my mind to the visit I had had at my friend Vanessa's home. Now, I was going to get to live in this kind of home.

The foster mom Diane was a widowed older lady who had been a foster parent for kids for many years. I shared a room with another foster child, Jetta, who was only six-years-old. As I looked at this little child, it reminded me that I was the same age as her when I was first sexually molested by my dad. I saw in her such innocence and hoped that she was not there for the same reasons that I was. I didn't know why she was there but assumed all kids in foster homes had been abused in one form or another.

Our room had two twin beds where we both had our own dressers and bedside tables with girly-like lamps on them. I barely had enough clothes to fill a grocery bag, never mind dresser drawers.

Jetta became so infatuated with me for some reason or another and loved to talk. Her questions came at me faster than I could answer them. "What's your name?" "How old are you?" and "Where are your mom and dad?", were just some of the initial questions when I first arrived. I was more interested in seeing the house that I would be living in. She was so excited and wanted me to be her friend. She would grab my hand and lead me on a detailed tour of the room we would share.

She opened the closest to show off her pretty clothes full of lacy little dresses befitting a little girl her age. There were so many of them, one that included a pink dress with a white collar. She had several pairs of patent leather shoes in the bottom of the closet, including a pair which reminded me of the pair I had gotten on the shopping trip with the officer so many years ago. It brought back a few fond memories, which were very rare in my lifetime.

Because she had such a gorgeous collection of clothes and shoes, I assumed she had been taken to the mall on numerous occasions. She pointed out some of her favorite outfits by reaching up to move the hangers from one side to the other. When I pulled out an outfit that I thought was cute she would change into it right away and model it for me.

There was another bedroom that had some of the most beautiful baby furniture that I had ever seen. There were two baby beds that had unstained bedding and cute little pillows of pastel greens and yellows suitable for baby girls or boys. There was a dresser in between the beds full of infant clothing and cloth diapers. There was baby powder, lotions, combs brushes, and a tiny set of fingernail clippers for easy access when caring for infants on the top of the dresser.

I looked around the room. I noticed a rocking chair in the corner, which sat beside a white draped bassinet. I began to hear the soft sounds of an infant waking up. I had no idea a baby was sleeping inside of it when I came into the room. A newborn baby was also living here, and she was only a few days old. Instinct kicked in as I walked over to the bassinet to reach down to pick her up. Diane told me to be careful as I picked up the infant and held her in my arms, stroking her little head. I said I thought she was probably waking up for her scheduled bottle feeding and a fresh diaper. This turned out to be correct.

I was all too willing and able to help with this newborn because I had brought years of experience with me. So, here I am, the newest member of this foster family, and beginning to feel very welcome. I wanted to find some kind of purpose in the pain I had been going through. This baby was the ice breaker that allowed me to feel like I had value here. I was happy to make her bottles, feed this tiny baby, and change her diapers because I had become a diaper changing pro. During the years of taking care of my siblings, I had mastered changing diapers without sticking the baby.

Diane took me to school and enrolled me in classes. She signed the forms, which asked me if I wanted to be considered for the cheerleading squad and if I was interested in being in the choir or any other extracurricular activities. I was never able to do any of these activities in the past. Diane also suggested to the office attendant that the administration should recommend a tutor for me. She recommended after school sessions that would help me catch up with some of the special programs they offered. I didn't understand why I needed a tutor but later discovered how very far behind I was in my grade level. She fully understood how important it was for me to be with kids my age and, therefore, did not want me placed in a lower grade.

This was a school like no other I had ever attended in the past. I was excited about all the attention I was getting. No one had ever taken an interest in my educational skills before "My Foster Mother." She made me feel special, like I had worth for the very first time in my life.

She told me to tell the students that she was my aunt to avoid the ridicule of being a foster kid. I am sure the school officials knew my background. Still, my foster mother, Diane, wanted me to experience being a normal teenager. So, I did, and I began making friends at the new school quickly. I had the newer clothes, the shoes that fit me well and were not falling apart. I began to blend into the kind of school life I never had before. The kids were treating me with respect, and my peers were accepting me.

There were no siblings here to remind me of the horrible life from which I came. I wondered and worried if they were being treated as well as this. They were always in the back of my mind. I wondered where they were all living and if my oldest brother was still staying at Eddie's. He hung out with them all the time anyway, so it would have been a good fit for him.

The bad experiences from my childhood were being replaced. My new life began to emerge. There were more surprises to come in the days ahead that rocked my world in ways I could never have known existed.

One of the girls in my class who lived on the same street as my foster home invited me to come over to her house to do our homework. I was eager to do my homework with her and was focused on getting good grades. I wanted to make my Foster Mother proud of me, and I didn't want to be the student who seemed to be overlooked because of bad grades. There were snacks on the table for us, and her mother sat with us and helped me understand the lessons in the books we were studying. It turns out she was the adult who was going to be my tutor! The patience she had with me was incredible. She didn't make me feel dumb or treat me any differently than she did her own daughter.

The cheerleaders at the many schools I had attended never talked to me, but here they were so welcoming, and the coach was so excited to add me to the squad as a substitute. Here, I could participate in after school activities that were never in the cards for me until now. The popular kids talked to me, and friendships formed as if I had known them all my life. I felt like a teenager, and for the first time, I felt proud as I walked through the halls alongside my new friends with my head held high as the former me began to disappear.

Cheerleading practices were scheduled later in the week after classes, and I was invited to attend. I would learn the routines and chants they used at ball games. Gosh, I remember watching cheerleaders practice in the gym in Searcy when Donna was doing her gymnastic activities on the big mats on the floor. I would sit in the bleachers and imagine what it would be like if I was a part of the squad, and now all of a sudden, here I was, living a dream.

I was raised in a life of despair, and I never saw a path like this for my future. I had been threatened by my dad about the horrors of living in foster homes as if they were the worst places I could be in. I didn't know how families lived beyond what I saw in the life of my own family, including my aunts and uncle. I caught a glimpse of a better way of life with my cousins in Pangburn and with my friend, Vanessa, the night I had spent at her home.

How did a poor kid like me end up with a life with hope? I wasn't sure at the time, but there would be more to discover in this life that I had accepted as being a path I was supposed to go down. I was taught how to do so many things that I didn't know that I had been doing wrong while growing up. It occurred to me that my natural mom had not taught us how to do basic tasks. She would only yell at us to do them and then yell at us again if we did them wrong.

My Foster Mother, who had become a real mother figure, was teaching me skills that I had no knowledge of. She taught me the right way to do dishes, and I no longer had to do the laundry. She cooked real meals for dinner that included meats, vegetables, and bread, and some items I had never eaten before. I told her I was used to eating "Hobo Bread"! With a squint in her eyes, she asked me what Hobo Bread was. After I described it to her, she chuckled and told me it sounded like a tortilla. I had not heard the term before, but it would always be known to me as Hobo Bread.

Diane was an active member of her local church. She would take the kids she had fostered over the years to church with her every Sunday morning. She took me to a Sunday School class, where I was welcomed with such grace and kindness. I was given a bible that had the old and new testaments with chapters I knew nothing about. I honestly didn't know how they referred to the books, chapters, and verses in a bible because we never experienced it at home.

In the chapel, a board on the wall listed the dollar amount of offerings from the prior Sunday and the page numbers of hymns that would be sung. I arrived at my place in the pew early, and I was able to mark the pages before the worship service began so that I could try to sing along. I didn't know any of the words of the hymns they sang nor the melody, but I sang along anyway. It was where I first heard "How Great Thou Art" and to this day, it is still my favorite hymn.

Diane taught me how to turn my bible to pages and read along as we sat in the pew. She helped me understand what was being said when the minister would quote books and chapters in the sermons that he was teaching. She read to us at home throughout the week, and a new path was starting to make sense to me.

In a few short weeks, I had entered into a real home environment. I enjoyed going to school. I had friends, teachers, and a church who helped me discover the power of God.

One Sunday, Diane invited me to go to her adult Sunday School class with her. I felt somewhat out of place, but once they started the class I felt more comfortable. Everyone was so accommodating to help me with the deeper level of bible studies and asked if I had questions. After the class ended, then it was time to take our spot in the pew. I felt very moved. I sang the hymns a little bit louder that day because I had a voice that I wanted to be heard.

As I listened to the sermon with such a level of attention this beautiful Sunday, I was amazed by his words that were being said more so than any of the other weeks before. I wasn't sure why I was more focused on this week's sermon. Perhaps, because it was the first time that I understood what the message was about, and I felt it deeply. It moved me in such a deep way that it was even more powerful than the one I felt when I had spent the night with Vanessa and prayed before dinner. This feeling was like no other I had ever felt before, and it is hard to explain why it was so strong. I sat there and listened to the message about how God can take away all the fears and pain in your life by accepting Jesus Christ, the son of God, into your heart. Then, he invited anyone who believed in the power of God to follow the path God had for them.

The minister then opened his arms and invited everyone to come down to the front to pray and accept God into their lives. He made me feel as if he was talking directly to me. I believed it was GOD talking to me, and I felt it! I was not going to let go of this feeling. Not this time! I wanted to have that kind of peace in my life. There was so much power in the room, I had to act on it. I looked up at my Foster Mother. At that moment, she was my mother, and I asked her if I could go down to the front of the altar. She looked at me and said, "That is a choice that only you could make." I felt the Holy Spirit moving through me in such a way, I got up from my seat, and I walked down the aisle of that little church. This poor, broken teenager, was accepted into their church family, and it was then and there that I gave my heart to God.

"I remember the chapel, the pews, the choir, every little detail!"

"GOD HAD A PATH FOR ME LONG BEFORE I EVER KNEW IT!"

All I had to do was accept Jesus Christ into my heart and let God clear the path he had prepared for me. *Protecting my family was now in his hands. I was free, and I found the peace I had longed for.*

I had lived a life of "CRYING WITHOUT TEARS!" It was then that I cried, and I was not able to stop crying. I felt like a huge burden had been lifted from me, and I could not hold back the tears. My church family was all crying with me! They were also celebrating the fact that I had made a choice by myself. This is who

I wanted to be, a child of GOD.

I didn't want my life to be defined by my past and what I had gone through. I wanted my life to be what God had planned for me.

The strength God had been giving me through all of those years was with me all along and I didn't even know it. We were all being raised in a house with no love and no faith. I was never taught how to pray, read a bible, or sing a simple hymn. Now I was being led down a path that I didn't know existed.

Just as importantly, God led me down the path of forgiveness. You must be able to truly forgive in order to set the past free. I had to find the strength to forgive my mom and dad, so I prayed very hard and eventually forgave them.

It started to make sense to me that the Chaplin who had prayed over me when I was so ill many years ago, and too young to understand what he was doing, was so clear to me now. He was using the power of God to heal me, and I did not even know it.

I felt in my heart that I had been there to protect the lives of my family from my mom and dad, who were "raising" us. Had I not been given the strength to finally say something to the authorities and give them "every little detail," our dad would have sexually abused the rest of his daughters. And mom did not have the power to stop him.

I didn't have a mother or father in the people who were raising me when I was young.

**I found my family in that little church,
my mother in a foster home,
and my father in God.**

God has given me the will and a path to tell my story. We can all be free with the power of God in our hearts.

I sincerely believe there was a reason I was placed in this home with Diane. Perhaps it was her innate ability to transform a broken teenager into being accepted by her peers at school. To be a friend to a little six-year-old girl or show me that no matter how bad life had been for me, now I could become respected in the community. Most importantly, she had faith in her home. The feeling was real, and I felt it from the first time I walked into her home, which became my home. Diane told me once that someday my new life would outshine the life I had left behind.

After foster home life, some of the older siblings and I found our way back to our family members in Indiana, including our mom. Call it maternal or closure, but we did as we aged out of the program. Some of the kids were adopted but we all reunited over the years. It was never the same. Seeing them all grown up was different for me. I took care of them as little kids and now they are adults.

We started to share stories about our childhood. As I talked to my younger sister Cathy, I discovered she had been sexually abused by an uncle and by the brother who stole all the time. She once asked him why he did some of the things he did. He replied, saying he didn't remember doing them. She asked him quite bluntly, *"Why can't you remember what I can't forget?"* He had no response and has ended up spending most of his life in jail. We all kind of saw that coming when we were kids.

She and I can now talk about the bad moments, but even more so, we laugh about some of the fun and stupid things we did when we were young. Kids will always be kids in any environment in which they are being raised.

My sister Donna Jean took her own life when she was 37 years old. She was never able to really find peace with what had happened to her as a child. She had always been a hard worker. She ultimately became a caregiver to our mom, the very person who had beaten her and told her many times that she hated her. All that she ever wanted was to be loved and accepted by her mother.

Some people have asked me how I was able to write about these terrible events. I just tell them GOD is leading me to share my story to help others. My message is not only how God came into my life, but to encourage others to recognize the signs of sexual, physical, or emotional abuse in children or adults.

It's up to us to lift them up and out of the life they are living. To teach them how GOD can change their path after abuse at any stage of their life. I found my peace with God!

I would share these words with any child who is being sexually abused, especially by a family member. Do not ever think it will just end. It will NOT. Seek out someone to help you. Trust in them and yourself because God puts people in your life for a reason. I had lived a life without crying, and although I was scared, I had given little signs here and there to the people around me.

NO ONE TOOK NOTICE!
NO ONE LISTENED!
HEAR ME NOW!

A Daughter's Perspective

Over my adult years I've heard portions of this harrowing experience and upbringing. Most of us would have crumbled and introverted as a result of what this woman went through as a child. But not my Mom! She chose her path to be one of survival, strength and mission. She is indeed the strongest overcomer I've ever known and admired. I know her heart remains true in helping raise awareness over this horrible reality.

Cheryl Renee Crowder
Cindy Spray's Daughter

Testimonies

What an inspiration for us who keep our tramatized feelings inside our "lock box" heart and minds.

Strong Soul. Strong Angel. And He gave her strength to survive and as our Shepard to lead for those in a weak valley. She climbed the mountain and was given strength. God Bless.

A. Ormsby

Cindy Spray's life story is shared by many, but spoken out by too few. God has endowed Cindy with a gift: the ability to share her life's darkest moments — even the things you wish you had not heard — while shedding light in the darkest of places and bringing hope to anyone who has suffered from being abused in the worst kind of ways. Through her life experiences shared in this book, God reveals to us how wonderful His grace is and how there's absolutely nothing we cannot overcome with Him on our side.

Renan DeBarros
DeBarros Ministries / Full Gospel Business Gatekeepers

Cindy's story is one of heartbreak and betrayal by those that she should have counted on for love and trust. I have known Cindy for 25 years and she has never let her abusive past define her or prevent her from accomplishing her goals. This book is a testament to her will and a testament to her faith in the Lord as our true savior and redeemer.

Mike Matthews

Wow! Words alone cannot explain the impact your story had on me. Your story of pain, neglect, shame, and uncertainty continued until one amazing foster mom opened her home and nurtured you. Your hungry heart was fed by her Love and Faith in God. I could almost feel your joy and absolute feeling of peace when you walked up to the altar and accepted Christ as your Savior! Your story will shine on as a beacon to others. Not only will it impact victims but open the eyes and ears of others to the atrocities of sexual abuse. I truly believe this factual account and your ability to forgive is a large part of God's plan for you.

Trudi S.

About the Author

Cindy, an Indiana "Hoosier" attended Indiana University where she studied Psychology. She later changed her goals and studied Accounting at Indiana Business College, while working at a local nonprofit as the Assistant Bookkeeper.

While there, she excelled in the accounting field, including serving as a co-chair in researching software programs to integrate a new bookkeeping system to better meet the needs of the business. She also assisted with implementing the employer's 401K program working with the Board of Directors.

She later focused on new endeavors in the manufacturing field with PepsiCo that included Purchasing, Logistic Maintenance, Manufacturing Maintenance and became instrumental in tracking equipment failures and the plants' conveyor belting systems.

Being involved with the high school mentorship program, she assisted senior students as they explored the opportunities the manufacturing field had to offer. She studied Spanish and became a tutor with the library literacy program teaching Hispanics to speak and read English.

Other interests included playing team tennis and volunteering as the Assistant Coach at the local high school on the Varsity and Jr Varsity teams and later became the Head Coach at another high school in the county for both the boys and girls teams. She represented her local tennis community in Indiana as Treasurer of the Frankfort Area Tennis Society "FATS" and became the director for the annual "Hotdog" tennis tournament that continues to be a favorite in the region.

With opportunities to be near family members became an option, she transferred to Bradenton, Florida and back to her accounting roots, ending her 20-year career with PepsiCo as the Senior Bookkeeper at the Tropicana Federal Credit Union where she maintained assets up to $26 million.

She now spends her free time with her husband Dave, family, gardening, and serves on local clubs, boards and committees as well as being involved with several nonprofits and charity programs.

A portion of the proceeds from the sale of this book will be donated to help foster care programs and bring awareness of child abuse and human trafficking networks that exist in our world.

Made in the USA
Columbia, SC
07 October 2021